My Real Mother

My Real Mother

Tina N. Katamay

Fabkat Enterprises
Paso Robles, California

Copyright © 2024 Tina N. Katamay
All Rights Reserved

Published by Fabkat Enterprises
Paso Robles, California

www.tinankatamay.com

Softcover ISBN: 979-8-218-35168-7

Hardcover ISBN: 979-8-218-35199-1

Ebook ISBN: 979-8-218-35200-4

This book is a reminiscence based on actual events. The names of the characters have been changed to preserve their anonymity.

This book and its contents are protected under International and Federal Copyright Laws and Treaties. Except for the quotation of short passages for the purpose of criticism or review, no part of this book may be reproduced or transmitted in any form or by any means, electronic or mechanical, including photocopying, recording, or by any information storage and retrieval system, without express written permission from the author.

Book designed and produced
by Lucky Valley Press
www.luckyvalleypress.com

Book cover art: @istock.com

Hands on the cover: Melanie and Ariah Moen

Author photo on page 173 by Kevin Richtik
@Caroline's Photography, Stockton CA

Printed in the USA on acid-free paper

Distributed globally by Ingram

Dedication

This book is dedicated to:
My sister Diana and my brother Ernie.
With you in mind I wrote *My Real Mother*, hoping you, and I,
would have a better understanding of our mother,
the child bride who never wanted to marry or have children
and longed for nothing more than to pursue her own dreams.

Contents

Acknowledgments vii

Foreword ix

Donald 1

The Wedding 15

Leaving Home 29

Gina 41

The Accident 55

The Sadness and the Sanitarium 61

Shock Treatment 69

Going Home 81

Vietnam 87

Hawaii 93

Joe 103

Trouble in Paradise 111

Kiana 123

Donald's Confession 131

Resuming Married Life 143

Without a Goodbye 155

The Final Betrayal 163

Epilogue 171

About the Author 173

Acknowledgments

First, I want to say thank you to my husband Roman and my daughter Amber for allowing me the time to write *My Real Mother*. Your sacrifices have been huge, and they are not unnoticed. I will be forever grateful for your love and support. Your loving words of encouragement have given me the courage to follow my dream of becoming a writer.

To my two amazing editors, Sandi and Ginna, thank you for being patient with me and lovingly guiding me through to the finish line. You are both blessings from God.

And, while there are numerous people I want to thank, there are too many to name individually. You know who you are and what you have given me along the way. I thank you for your patience. I hope you like *My Real Mother* and that it was worth the wait.

Foreword

When I set out to write *My Real Mother* I did not know where to begin. However, my mother's last words were, "Now write the book."

Now write the book she and I joked about writing for years.
Now write the book and share with the world the truth about her betrayal to her husband, to her children, and to herself.
Now write the book that could answer all my questions.

How? My mother was dead. The truth died with her, still she'd given me her blessing to write the book. I felt helpless to write it alone though because she had given me so little truth to go on. Determined, I tried. I sat for hours in front of my computer typing, but nothing rang true. Had it ever? Her stories, her lies, her fabrications…

Finally, frustrated, I cried out, saying, "Momma, if you want me to write this book, then you'll have to help me," to which I heard in her sweet southern drawl, "Well darlin', if we are gonna tell this story, then I think we better start at the beginnin'."

Donald

It was a Wednesday night in 1957, at the First Baptist Church on Main Street, in the small town of Fresno, California. Linda Hall was sitting in the last row, having no idea what the message had been about because she daydreamed through most of it.

It was only the sound of the church's pianist playing "How Great Thou Art" that drew her attention back to the present. Instinctively, she rose to sing the closing hymn with all the other parishioners, then she bowed her head as the Pastor led the closing prayer. When his prayer concluded, Pastor Ron asked, "Okay, with every head bowed and with every eye closed, I want a show of hands. Who here has accepted Jesus Christ as their personal savior?"

Since she'd accepted Jesus into her heart at Bible camp last summer, her hand shot up proudly. Curious to see who else had raised their hand, keeping her head bowed, Linda opened her eyes and looked to her left.

The blood rushing to her head drowned out the rest of Pastor Ron's altar call because there sat the most handsome boy she'd ever seen. His hand was up, his head bowed slightly, both of his eyes were wide open, and he was staring straight at her. Mortified he'd caught her peeking, Linda quickly closed her eyes and prayed silently, *Dear God, please forgive me.*

After the meeting, Linda was at the refreshment table when the same young man walked up to her. Putting out his hand, he said, "Hi, my name's Donald Holloway. What's your name, beautiful?" he asked.

He smiled and Linda's heart raced, her face flushed, and her knees wobbled a bit.

Accepting his hand, she answered, "My name's Linda Hall."

"*Well*, Linda Hall," Donald said, "I think we should go for a soda on Sunday."

It was more of a statement than a question and, not knowing what else to say, Linda responded, "I don't think my daddy would allow it. Besides, we go to church on Sundays," she added.

"Then I'll ask your daddy if I can take you for a soda after church on Sunday," he said.

"*Well*, Donald Holloway," Linda said, "I'll tell you what. If I decide I wanna go for a soda with you, I'll ask my daddy and let you know."

Later, lying in bed, Linda blushed deeply, remembering Donald calling her beautiful. No one had ever called her beautiful before. In fact, being on the tomboyish side, none of the boys at church or anywhere else for that matter had given Linda so much as a second look. And, while she may have sounded disinterested, the thought of going for a soda with Donald excited her in a terrifying kind of way.

Unaware this night was going to be the one that changed Linda's life forever, she drifted off to sleep, smiling.

* * *

The next day Linda was upstairs in her bedroom, lying on her bed doing homework, when she heard a knock on the front door. Too lazy to get up and walk to the door, her brother William yelled from the couch, "Yeah, what'd you want?"

Hearing the familiar voice say, "I'm here to ask Mr. Hall if I can take Linda out for a soda after church this Sunday," Linda sat up in shock.

"Hey, Daddy," William yelled again, "There's a boy at the door asking if he can take Linda for a soda on Sunday!"

Sitting on the edge of her bed, Linda heard her daddy get up from the table and walk to the front door. She held her breath, hoping to hear what they said but she couldn't hear a thing because her daddy had closed the door behind him.

* * *

In the Hall house, dinner was always eaten in silence, However, that night her daddy broke his own rule, saying, "Linda, a boy came a callin' here today askin' if he could take you for a soda on Sunday."

Sitting between her parents, Linda looked first at her momma, then her daddy, but said nothing.

"How do you know this boy?" her daddy asked.

"I met him at church last night," Linda answered.

"Do you wanna go for a soda with him?" he asked.

"I don't know. I ain't given it much thought," Linda answered. Which was a lie, because she thought of nothing else all day.

"Linda, what do you know about this boy?" her momma asked.

"I know his name is Donald, but that's all I know."

Looking at her daddy, her momma said, "I don't think she should go."

Somewhat relieved, Linda said, "I never said I wanted to go."

"Well, I think she should go," her daddy said. "He seems like a nice enough young man, and she is the next in line to marry off."

Indignant, and forgetting the original subject all together, Linda asked, "What do you mean I'm the next one to be married off?"

Getting up from the table, her daddy said, "I've said my piece, I'm goin' to the bar," and walked away.

Following her daddy out of the room, her momma said, "Linda, William's having dinner at the Russell's tonight. I'm gonna need you to sit with Arnie."

Under her breath, Linda said, "Don't I always?"

After her parents left, Linda washed the dinner dishes, pouting. Ever since her older sister got married, Linda had to watch her much younger brother on the nights her momma and daddy went to the bar, which seemed to be more often these days.

It was laughable because having to watch Arnie was why she started going to church on Wednesday nights. What started out as a weekly reprieve now felt like a curse.

It was confusing, because if Linda had money to bet, she would've put it all on her daddy saying she couldn't go on a date with Donald, while her momma argued she may as well go because she'd have to date eventually if she was going to find a husband. Could it be her daddy really wanted her gone? Married off, as he put it?

And what about her momma? Why wouldn't she want me to go on a date? She always said it was a woman's duty to marry. Wasn't this the next obvious step to fulfilling her duty?

Linda sighed heavily, wondering what in the world she was going to do about Donald as the anger welled up inside her, realizing her momma just wanted a babysitter so she could go to the bar with her daddy.

* * *

When Linda walked out of church the following Sunday, Donald was standing across the street, next to his car, waiting for her. Since the subject of going for a soda with Donald hadn't come up again, Linda looked around for her parents for some direction.

She saw her daddy first. He was standing on the far side of the church in a group of men passing around what looked like a whiskey bottle.

Waving her arms frantically until she got his attention, Linda looked back at Donald, then at her daddy and shrugged her shoulders.

With a quirky smile, her daddy shrugged his shoulders leaving the decision to her.

Linda had to admit the idea seemed exciting, but as she walked toward Donald, her legs felt heavy. Her head screamed STOP. Her legs didn't listen.

Like a cow to slaughter, she thought. *Dear God, Linda, what made you think of something like that?* With no time to ponder the question, she approached the car just as Donald opened the driver's door, and mechanically Linda climbed in, sliding across to the passenger side.

Riding in a car alone with a boy who wasn't her brother with no momma and no daddy anywhere in sight, suddenly Linda felt so grown up.

After parking the car, Donald got out, ran around to the other side, and opened the door for her. Looking up at Donald, Linda smiled nervously and said, "Thank you."

Inside, Donald ordered two root beers and a basket of fries. In a nearby booth they sat across from each other in silence.

Finding her voice first, Linda asked, "How'd you find out where I live?"

Throwing his head back laughing, Donald asked, "Does it matter?"

"It does to me," she answered, upset he was laughing at her.

"I hope you won't be mad at me. I followed you home after church," Donald said.

Sounding angrier than she felt, Linda said. "You should've let me ask my daddy."

"If you asked, he would've said no, for sure," Donald said.

"I never said I wanted to have a soda with you, and I distinctly remember saying if I decided I did, I'd ask my daddy myself. Did you forget about that?" Linda asked.

Donald's eyes changed, hardening a bit. It was just for a second, but it was long enough for Linda to notice, and it made her feel uncomfortable.

"Well, we're here now, and that's what matters," Donald said.

She remembered the moment she opened her eyes during prayer and saw the way he was looking at her. There was just something that made her feel uncomfortable. Try as she might though, Linda couldn't put her finger on what.

Hoping to change the subject, Linda said, "Thank you for the soda."

Appearing fully recovered, Donald smiled, saying, "You're welcome," then asked, "Would you like to go for a ride in my car?" which nearly caused Linda to choke on her soda. Her daddy never said she could go riding around in a car, but then again, her daddy had left it up to her. So, giving the question one second's thought, she answered, "Sure, why not?" Linda answered. "Can I listen to the country radio station?"

Back in the car, excited, she asked again, "Can I listen to the radio?" Without waiting for an answer, she flipped it on, turned the dial to the station her daddy listened to at home, and proceeded to sing her heart out as Donald drove out of town toward the lake.

A few minutes later, Donald pulled over, turned off the ignition and said, "Wow, you have a beautiful voice. Where did you learn to sing like that?"

"No one taught me," Linda said. "I just always loved to sing. So, whenever I get the chance, I sing."

Linda was tempted to tell Donald the secret she had told no one, not even Mabel—that she had always dreamed of singing on the big stage one day. Singing, all dolled up in a pretty dress, just like those lady singers she saw on her daddy's TV. Afraid he'd laugh at her again, she didn't tell him.

As a child, Linda loved to wander off and find a secluded spot where, with a stick in hand, she'd sing any song that came to mind. School songs, church songs, songs she heard on the country station. It didn't matter; she sang them all. Even if she didn't know all the words, she'd make some up. She remembered hiding behind a barn or a building, singing her heart out. With her eyes closed, she pretended she was singing on a stage in front of lots of people. With each note she sang, Linda flew higher and higher.

Moved by the passion of the lyrics, her body would sway to the emotion her voice conveyed, singing from the depths of her soul.

Abruptly, Donald asked, "Have you ever been kissed?"

Surprised, Linda nodded her head yes, admitting she had been kissed before. Okay, maybe it was a quick peck on the mouth by a first cousin, but it was a kiss.

Then, before she knew what was happening, Donald's mouth was on hers, forcing her lips apart as he pushed his tongue into her mouth. Pulling away, she shouted, "DEAR GOD, NO! I ain't ever been kissed like that before!"

Donald threw his head back, laughing at her again. Linda couldn't see the humor in any of it, still she laughed nervously with him. She truly hadn't meant to yell, but his kiss both frightened and fascinated her all at the same time.

Opening the glove compartment, Donald pulled out a pack of cigarettes, offering her one. Still reeling from the kiss, Linda looked at the cigarette and said, "No, thank you."

"What, you haven't ever smoked, either?" Donald asked, with the emphasis on the word either.

Linda shook her head as she watched Donald light two cigarettes at once. Handing her one, he asked, "Want to try it?"

Not wishing to hear Donald laugh at her again, Linda took the cigarette. Holding it nervously between her first two fingers, raising it to her lips, she took a drag, inhaled deeply, and immediately began coughing.

Again, Donald laughed, making Linda madder.

"If you're such an expert, why don't you show me how it's done." Linda snapped.

"Technically, you're supposed to do it exactly like you did. Here, watch me," Donald said.

Linda watched as Donald showed her how to smoke a cigarette. She tried again, inhaling slowly, then exhaling a huge plume of smoke, thankful this time she didn't choke.

For the next hour, Linda listened as Donald talked, mostly about himself. Knowing it was getting late, Linda said, "I better be getting home. Daddy'll be worried."

"Okay," Donald said, kissing her sweetly on the cheek. "We better get you home then. We wouldn't want to upset your daddy."

When Donald pulled up to the curb, Linda jumped out of the car and ran to the front porch. Turning back, she waved goodbye, forgetting she was ever mad.

Opening the front door as quietly as she could, praying her momma wouldn't hear her, Linda headed straight for the stairs.

Following her, her momma yelled, "Linda, wait a minute. How was the soda?"

"It was fine, Momma," Linda answered, yelling back over her shoulder. Racing to her bedroom, Linda grabbed the doorknob and tried to close the door quickly, but her momma was quicker.

Pushing back on the door, her momma asked, "Where did ya'll go?"

"Oh my gosh, Momma," Linda said, "we went to the Frosties. Why?"

"I'm just curious, that's all," her momma answered.

"Okay, like I said, we went to Frosties. We drank root beer and talked, that's all."

"What do you mean, 'that's all'?" her momma asked.

"It means there's nothing else to tell," Linda answered, closing the door.

Alone in her room, she sat on the edge of her bed, remembering the feel of Donald's lips against hers, her body tingling from head to toe with an odd sense of longing.

* * *

By the time Donald and Linda had been dating for six months, she was proficient at both kissing and smoking.

She and Donald were together before and after school, at the Friday night football games, and even Sundays at church.

They were together so much Linda couldn't remember her life before Donald. And maybe because he complimented momma on her cooking, something daddy never did, Donald had even grown on her momma. Sometimes, her parents allowed Donald to stay after dinner while they went to the bar. Donald and Linda would sit in the living room watching

TV with Arnie unless her brother William was home. If William was home, they would pawn Arnie off on him and sit in front of the house in Donald's car, kissing until they steamed up the windows.

Skipping school was something else Linda hadn't done before either, but when Donald said he had something important to tell her that couldn't wait, curious, she agreed to skip class with him. They drove to the lake, found a very secluded place and because the day was warm, they stripped down to their underwear and jumped into the water to cool off. Linda swam as hard as she could, trying to put distance between them. Donald out-swam her easily.

Swimming back to shore laughing at their antics, Linda was about to get out of the water when Donald grabbed her arm and pulled her back in. Spinning her around, he kissed her long and hard. Unable to breathe, Linda pulled away. Climbing out of the water, she picked up her dress and quickly put it on.

Walking over to the car, she sat down in the front seat rubbing her bruised arms, wishing Donald would get on with telling her his important news.

Donald followed a few minutes later, and as Linda watched Donald pull on his pants, she noted his eyes were fixed intently on her. His stare annoyed her.

"Why are you looking at me like that?" Linda asked.

Not taking his eyes off her, Donald said, "There's something I need to tell you."

Brushing her hair out with her fingers. Linda said, "I'm listenin'."

When Donald still didn't speak, Linda said, "For heaven's sake, Donald, what is it? Your makin' me nervous."

Then, shocked, she stopped brushing in mid-stroke when Donald said, "I've quit school."

"What? Why would you do that?" she asked.

"Because I'm going into the Army," he answered. "You know the United States is going to get into the war in Vietnam eventually and I want to be ready."

Sternly, Linda said, "Just because there's a war goin' on doesn't mean you gotta quit school and join up now. You'll probably get drafted after you graduate, anyway."

Grabbing her again by the arms, this time more gently, Donald said, "Linda, this is something I've got to do. Please try to understand."

Linda sat silently absorbing the news, not knowing how she felt about it or even how his decision to quit school and join the Army affected her.

"Are you ever coming back to Fresno?" she asked.

"Of course," he said, "boot camp's only for six weeks, then I'll be back."

She was staring out the window, trying to sort out her feelings, when Donald produced a little diamond ring.

"Linda, will you marry me?" Donald asked.

"For cryin' out loud, Donald," Linda said, "I'm only fifteen years old. I ain't old enough to be marryin' no one."

Laughing, Donald said, "People get married young all the time, Linda."

That's true, Linda said.

Her sister was only seventeen when she got married. And even her momma and daddy got married young. *Still*, she thought, *just because people do, don't mean I gotta.*

Holding the ring up, Donald asked, "Linda, will you marry me?"

"Donald, you know my daddy ain't gonna allow it," she said.

"You thought he wouldn't let us date either." Donald said. "I will ask him,"

It wasn't that Linda didn't enjoy being with Donald; she did. Most of the time.

With sad eyes, Donald asked, "You love me, don't you?"

She certainly loved riding around in his car and kissing, she really liked that! The thought of him going away made her feel sad, but was that love? Did she love Donald? Linda wasn't sure.

Then Donald asked again, this time louder, "Linda, do you love me?"

Linda knew she needed time to consider her feelings, but not wanting to hurt Donald's feelings, she whispered, "I don't know Donald, maybe I do."

Grabbing the blanket Donald kept on the back seat, Linda got out of the car and walked over to a nearby tree and spread it out. She sat down and lit a cigarette.

A few minutes later, Donald sat down next to her and gently pulled her over to him, kissing her face, her neck, her ears, and her mouth.

"Please stop, Donald." Linda said, trying to get up. His kisses were heady, and she felt like she was drowning. "Donald, stop. You're driving me crazy, I need to think," she said, pushing him away.

Donald didn't stop. He became forceful, pushing her down, forcing his way on top of her. Then, placing his knee between hers, she felt him push as if trying to spread her legs apart. Scared, Linda pushed back hard.

"Donald!" Linda yelled, "I said stop!"

She watched uncomfortably as Donald's eyes went from hard to near tears in a flash.

"Oh, Linda," Donald said, "I'm so sorry, please forgive me. I got carried away when you said you love me. I didn't mean to hurt to you." When she did not respond, Donald begged, "Linda, please don't be mad at me. I love you and I want to marry you."

"I didn't say I love you. I said maybe I do," Linda whispered.

Gently kissing her cheek, Donald buried his face in her neck. Feeling the warmth of his breath upon her skin, Linda's head spun.

"That's good enough for me," Donald whispered. "Please say you'll marry me."

So, with his kisses exciting her young tender body and his words wooing her tender heart, Linda whispered, "Okay, if my daddy says yes, I will marry you."

When they pulled up in front of her parents' house, Donald jumped out of the car and ran around to the passenger side. Opening the door, he pushed the little diamond ring into her hand and whispered in her ear, "Don't tell anyone about our plans yet."

Thankful no one was home, Linda ran up the stairs, threw herself on her bed, and cried. She felt so confused. Was it love she felt when Donald kissed her?

Finally, all cried out, she lay staring at the ceiling, remembering the feel of Donald's body on top of hers. She could still feel the warmth of his hands where he'd touched her bare skin. The memory caused a warm sensation that started at her feet, running up her legs, over her knees and exploding between her thighs, causing a pulsating sensation Linda knew nothing of.

All of her life, her momma told her one day she'd get married and have babies because that's what women do. What her momma hadn't done was take the time to explain how you went from getting married to having babies. Somehow, Linda felt sure it had something to do with the pulsating sensation she felt down there.

* * *

One week later, Linda was sitting on the front porch swing waiting for Donald when her daddy walked outside and sat down next to her.

"So, what are you and Donald up to tonight?" he asked.

Not sure if it was true, Linda answered, "Going to a movie."

When Donald pulled up, Linda jumped up intending to run out to meet him, but her daddy grabbed her by the arm saying, "Sit yourself down, missy. You wait for your young man to come and get you."

Just then, her momma walked out onto the porch and Linda jumped up again, this time to give momma her place on the porch swing, next to her daddy.

Running down the front steps, Linda yelled, "We better get goin'. We don't wanna to be late for the movie."

As Donald got closer, Linda could see his face was pale, and he didn't look so good. She felt her own dinner rise from her stomach into her throat because the look on Donald's face said it all.

He never looked at her, just her parents. First, he looked at her momma, "Good evening, ma'am," Donald said. Then he turned to her daddy and, without taking a pause, Donald said, "Mr. Hall, I'd like your permission to marry Linda."

Linda held her breath, silently praying her daddy'd say no.

Clearing his throat, her daddy looked at her momma and said, "You two are awfully young to marry. Ya'll haven't even finished your schooling yet. How about you tell us your plans, son?"

"That's all true sir," Donald said. "However, I've joined the Army. I leave for boot camp in a week, and with your permission, I'd like for us to get married before I leave."

Linda's head snapped up in surprise and she blurted out, "Wait, what's the rush? I wanna finish school," Linda said, but nobody was listening to her.

Without even looking Linda's way, Donald continued, saying, "And of course, Linda can finish the school year and I'll come for her when I get stationed somewhere permanent."

"Donald, we ain't talked about any of this. We need to talk," Linda begged, tugging on his arm. Donald stood ramrod stiff, looking at her daddy, waiting for his answer.

"Daddy, me and Donald need to talk," Linda said, pulling on Donald's shirt sleeve. Donald shook her off, not taking his eyes off her daddy. What she heard next was the biggest shock of all. Without even asking if she wanted to marry Donald, her daddy said, "Congratulations son, I hope ya'll get stationed somewhere close by." then getting up, he walked into the house, closing the door behind him.

"Donald, Linda said, I think I'll pass on goin' out tonight. I don't feel so good," then she turned and followed her daddy into the house.

In her room, standing in front of her dresser staring at herself in the mirror, she wondered what in the world just happened? In the past twenty minutes, she'd gone from a schoolgirl about to go on a date to being engaged to a boy she barely knew.

She'd been so sure her daddy'd say no. And why hadn't her momma spoken up? It was just a few months ago her momma was against her and Donald even dating.

Nothing made any sense. For God's sake, she was only 15 years old. Was she the only one who realized they were just kids? Or maybe it had been her daddy's intention all along, to marry her off like he said.

Jumping off her bed angrily, Linda threw open her bedroom door, intending to confront her parents, when she heard them yelling downstairs.

Their fighting was another thing occurring more and more lately. Tiptoeing down the stairs, Linda sat at the bottom, listening.

And although she didn't find out why her daddy gave his permission for them to get married, she did find out her daddy had lost his job weeks ago. Linda quit listening when her momma asked where her daddy had been spending his days and her daddy didn't answer. She didn't care to know the answer to that question.

* * *

Linda was barely awake the next morning when her momma walked in and sat down on the edge of her the bed, saying, "So, as of last night you're officially a woman."

Linda burst out laughing, "Seriously, Momma? I'm fifteen years old and I ain't no more a woman today than I was yesterday."

Putting up her hand to silence Linda, her momma said, "You are almost sixteen years old and you're engaged now. Which means you're about to be Donald's wife and soon you'll be havin' his babies."

"Momma, please listen," Linda pleaded. "I don't wanna be no one's wife."

"No Linda, you to listen to me," her momma scolded. "You need to marry Donald and get the hell out of here. Your Daddy told me last night he lost his job, again. If he doesn't find work soon, we'll be back to living in the damned car."

Raising her voice, Linda said, "I don't understand why that's a problem. Daddy's lost his job lots of times and we've moved more times than I can count, but we ain't never had to get rid of a kid before."

"Linda, we've always struggled, you know that. The truth is both Howard and Mabel left home knowin' it was the best thing for the family."

"Howard left because he didn't like daddy's drinkin', Momma. And Mabel left when she got married," Linda argued.

Linda knew things had always been hard for her parents. There never was enough money, but she didn't see how her getting married was going to help much.

"I am sorry you feel like we're gettin' rid of you. Please try to understand. Your daddy feels Donald can take better care of you than he can, and he thinks this is the best thing for you."

"What do you think, Momma?" Linda asked.

"I think Donald goin' into the Army is a good thing. There will be a steady income. You'll always have a home and there will be money to buy nice things. Don't you want nice things?" her momma asked.

Linda hadn't ever given it much thought, but answered, "I guess so." Wiping the tears from her eyes, she asked, "Still, I wanna know if you think marryin' Donald is the best thing for me, Momma?"

With tears in her eyes, her Momma answered, "I ain't gonna sugar coat things, Linda, marriage ain't always easy but, yes, I think your marryin' Donald is for the best,"

Getting married and having babies wasn't what Linda wanted.

She just wanted to sing.

Wondering if maybe there was still a way she could sing on the big stage and be a wife too, for the next half hour, Linda listened as her momma told her, in some detail, what she could expect on her wedding night.

When her momma finished speaking, she asked, "Do you have any questions?"

With the tears now streaming down her face, Linda asked, "Is it gonna hurt?"

"Yes, but only for a minute," her momma answered.

When her momma left the room, Linda laid on her bed, thinking about everything she'd said. Linda still wasn't sure marrying Donald was the best thing for her, however she could read between the lines and understood her marrying Donald was the best thing for her family. And she was very curious about what her momma called, "the coming together of a husband and a wife."

The Wedding

In just a few days' time, Linda sat in the front seat of Donald's car as they drove to City Hall. Making sure they'd adhered to all the wedding day rituals, her momma insisted Linda have something old, something new, something borrowed, and something blue. For the old, there was her dress. Something new, the shiny engagement ring on her left hand. The borrowed were her momma's shoes and Donald's car was her something blue. There hadn't been time to invite friends or family, so her momma was both her only guest and her witness. Donald's father, Irwin, volunteered to be his witness and was sitting in the back seat with her momma. Linda did not know where her daddy was.

At the courthouse, in her Sunday best, a three-year-old, one size too small quarter length cream colored dress with tiny satin embroidery around the neck, Linda stood numb with her momma on her right and Donald on her left. The sirens in her head were so loud they drowned out the sound of her voice as she promised to love, honor, and cherish Donald. She heard Donald say, "I do," and when prompted, she did, too. When Donald reached for her hand, her first thought was to pull away. Instead, she stared down at her hand as Donald slipped a gold wedding band next to the tiny diamond engagement ring.

She heard the clerk say, "I now pronounce you husband and wife. Mr. Holloway, you may kiss your bride." She felt Donald kissing her lightly on her mouth, sealing the deal. Like a spectator more than a participant, Linda watched as her momma rushed over and hugged her. She saw Irwin pat Donald on the back, congratulating his son. Then the room started to spin, and the next thing Linda felt was her head hit the floor as her world went black.

When she came to, she was lying flat on her back, staring up at the ceiling. Donald knelt next to her, looking worried, and her momma was crying.

Sitting up slowly, embarrassed, Linda asked, "Can we leave now, please?"

Once again, the four of them piled into the car. Linda did not know where they were going, but she was starving and hoped it was in pursuit of food.

Pulling up in front of her momma and daddy's house, Linda was about to reach for the door handle when Donald said, "Wait here. I'll be right back."

"Wait here? Why, where are you goin'?" Linda asked.

"To walk Pa to his truck. Then we can leave," Donald answered.

Puzzled, Linda asked, "Leave? Where are we goin'?"

Smiling, Donald said, "Just up the road a bit, to a motel."

"Oh, of course," she said, looking down and fiddling with her wedding ring.

Linda was waiting like she was told to when her momma walked up and handed her a small suitcase, saying, "I've packed everything you'll need in here."

"Thank you," was all Linda could say with tears in her eyes. She felt like a puppet. All day long, she'd just followed along.

Stand here, say this, wait here, take this and she wondered if this wasn't just the beginning of a lot of directions she was going to have to follow.

"Hello," Donald said, waving his hand in front of her face.

"Huh, what? I'm sorry. Did you say something?" Linda asked.

"Yes, I asked if you're hungry?"

Happy for the diversion, Linda answered, "Yes, I'm starvin'."

* * *

A half hour later, they stopped at a roadside restaurant. Being from a poor family with five children, they hadn't eaten out often, so going to a restaurant was always a treat and it lifted Linda's spirits immensely and for a while, she stopped worrying about what lay ahead. Sitting in the corner booth, they ordered hamburgers and fries. They drank milkshakes, talking and taking turns picking out songs on the tabletop jukebox. To Linda it felt just like any other date night.

After they'd finished eating, Donald lit two cigarettes and handed one to Linda, which she gladly accepted.

Closing her eyes, she leaned back and took a long deep drag, listening to Donald talk about what he called their "plans for the future." The last thing Linda wanted to think about was the future. What future? Right now, her future looked bleak. Donald would have his job. What about her?

Then Donald mentioned kids and Linda's eyes flew open.

"I assume you want kids someday," he said.

Growing up, Mabel and Linda talked about having babies one day. Mabel had always wanted them, but Linda wasn't sure. "I don't know. I ain't thought much beyond tonight. Why? Do you?" she asked.

Laughing in classic Donald style, he answered, "Yes, at least a dozen."

With wide eyes, Linda said, "I seriously hope you're joking."

"Of course, I'm joking, but one day we will have babies," Donald said.

Dear God, was that her future? Momma told her repeatedly it was her duty to get married and have babies, just like she and her grandma had.

Linda didn't want her momma's life. No, a life of cooking, cleaning, and having babies did not suit her. Linda wanted more than that. She wanted to sing.

"I think we should get going now. The motel's not far," Donald said.

The last two hours had been so enjoyable Linda wasn't ready for it to end. She knew even though it might've felt like any other date night, tonight was different. Tonight, she wasn't going home.

Parked in the motel parking lot, Donald said, "Wait here. I'll be right back." And true to his word, a few minutes later Donald returned, smiling.

His smile quickly disappeared. Looking concerned, he asked, "Is something wrong?"

"No. Why?" Linda lied.

"Because you're as white as a sheet," Donald answered. "Are you okay?" he asked.

Unable to answer, Linda reached for the door handle and was about to get out of the car when Donald grabbed her by the arm, saying, "Wait, I have something to say."

Feeling sick to her stomach, Linda said, "Go ahead, but please hurry."

"I want you to know, um," Donald said, "I won't hurt you."

Linda knew Donald was talking to her, but she heard nothing as scenes from the last few months flashed before her eyes. She remembered the moments when the excitement of Donald's kisses had been almost too much to bear. And the times they'd almost crossed an unspoken line. Her heart beat fast as she remembered Donald's hand touching her breast through her blouse. Feeling cold, she crossed her arms, covering herself. She remembered their last encounter, too, just a couple of weeks ago, when Donald had been rough and forceful. She waited for that fear to return. It didn't. "Can we just go to our room now, please?" Linda asked.

As Donald opened the door, Linda crossed the threshold to their room carrying her momma's suitcase and walked straight into the bathroom. Closing the door behind her, she leaned back against it and lowered herself to the floor. One minute excited, knowing this time when they kissed, they wouldn't stop; the next, terrified, knowing this time when they kissed, they wouldn't stop. She also knew she couldn't sit on the bathroom floor all night, so Linda dragged the suitcase over to her.

Opening it, she found a white silk nightgown right on top. It was lacy and looked expensive. She lifted it to her face, feeling it against her skin, inhaling the scent of it. It was so silky soft and smelled like her momma.

Attached to it with a straight pin was a note:

Dearest Daughter,

I pray you'll forgive your daddy and me. We only want the best for you. I hope you'll find happiness and contentment in your life with Donald. Remember, not all roads are easy, but they are what you make them. It's up to you. Now, go to your husband. Love, Momma.

Before Linda felt ready, dressed in her momma's nightgown, she opened the bathroom door. Her hair was down and she stood barefoot, shivering in the doorway, wondering what she was supposed to do next.

As if reading her mind, Donald stood up and opened his arms wide. Freezing, she crossed her arms over her almost fully exposed breasts and ran to him. She instantly felt warmer. As Donald held her in his arms and she noticed he was shaking. Linda hadn't even considered Donald might be nervous, too.

"Come, get warm," Donald said.

Pulling back the covers, Linda slid quickly into the bed and drew the covers up to her chin while Donald undressed, never taking his eyes off her. Linda watched with wide-eyed curiosity, unable to look away, and by the time he was done, Linda no longer felt cold.

Donald turned out the light before crawling into bed beside her. In the dark, she felt braver as Donald reached out and pulled her toward him.

Donald's kisses and caresses were nothing like before, neither sweet and searching, nor hot and demanding. They were clumsy. And before Linda could say anything, Donald was on top of her probing, pushing, and searching, but not finding what he looked for. He seemed upset. Not sure if she was supposed to or not, Linda reached down to help him.

Then a flash of light exploded inside her head as pain shot through the lower half of her body but, as quickly as it came, the pain faded, and Donald began caressing her from the inside with a gentle rhythm. It amazed her that her body instinctively knew what to do. Moving together rhythmically, each move took her higher and higher. Then, as quickly as it began, it was over. And before long, Donald was sound asleep.

Linda lay in the dark, listening to the sound of gentle snoring beside her. Unable to sleep, she got up and lit a cigarette. Letting the glow of the cigarette light her way, she walked over and sat down on the well-worn couch under the window. Reaching for the plastic wand, she drew back the faded plastic curtains covering the dirty window and looked out. The light posts in the parking lot cast a murky yellow glow on everything it touched.

Linda sat bathed in the same grim yellow light, remembering the feel of Donald rocking her body. Remembering the feel of him inside of her caused her body temperature to rise again. She first felt the heat on her face. Then it ran down her neck, over her silk clad breast, and like a bolt of lightning, exploded between her clenched knees.

Before long shivering, Linda crushed out her cigarette and ran back to the warmth of the bed. And as the emotions of the day washed over her, exhausted, she slept.

* * *

The next morning, they were up early. They packed quickly, climbed into the car, and left the motel, neither of them mentioning the night before. After finding another roadside restaurant, they were just about to eat when Donald said, "I have a surprise. I'm taking you home to meet my mother," and suddenly Linda lost her appetite.

As they drove further and further north, Linda's first thought was to beg Donald to take her home, but the idea of a road trip sounded fun. So, sitting next to Donald with the windows rolled down and the car radio up, Linda relaxed.

She'd forgotten how much she loved being in a car and soon felt chatty and shared some stories of her family on the road in their beat-up old station wagon. Laughing, Linda said, "You know daddy, he'd get a wild hair, and off we'd go into the blue yonder." Somehow, her life of moving from state to state, and town to town, or even living in the back seat of their car, didn't seem so bad when she joked about it.

As they talked, laughed, smoked, and sang along with the radio, it was easy to forget they were really married. It seemed just like any other day to Linda and besides the slight bruising between her thighs, nothing seemed any different.

* * *

A short time later, they pulled up in front of an older, quaint, two-story house with a neatly manicured yard.

Two blue metal chairs, one on each side of the front door, added a sweet touch to the house's charm. Donald was just getting out of the car when Linda saw the screen door fly open and a woman come running down the stairs toward them with her eyes firmly focused on Donald.

Linda watched as Donald opened his arms and his mother ran into them. He picked her up and swung her around. Setting her back down, he asked, "How are you, Ma?"

Linda saw her mother-in-law's features change. It was just for a split second, but she was sure she saw sadness there.

Recovering quickly, she answered, "I'm fine."

Donald must've seen it too because he asked again, "How are you, Ma?"

She turned and looked sternly at Donald, saying, "Like I said, I'm fine. Don't worry yourself about me," Myra said. Then she asked, "How are you, Donny boy?"

"Never better," Donald answered. Placing his arm around Linda's shoulder, Donald said, "Linda, this is my mother, Myra."

Linda looked at Myra and received a warm smile.

"Ma, this is my wife, Linda," Donald said. Linda saw the brief shock on her mother-in-law's face, but again, Myra recovered quickly. Saying "Welcome to the family," hugging Linda sweetly.

Myra's hands felt rough on Linda's shoulders. Her skin was dark and beautifully weathered. She wore a plain dress with a white apron. Her jet-black hair was short.

She seemed nice enough, and Linda relaxed at once. Inside the house, Myra introduced Linda to Donald's stepfather, James, and his two stepbrothers, George Jr. and Eldon.

Since lunch was ready, they went straight to the table. The conversation flowed freely between Donald and his parents about things she knew nothing of, so Linda paid little attention. Instead, she focused on the food. Unlike her momma's beans, Myra cooked hers with bacon, served with rice instead of cornbread, and paper thin tortillas. Linda ate several smothered in butter.

When the conversation turned to their wedding again, Linda noticed the sadness on her mother-in-law's face.

"I wish I'd known you were getting married. I would've been there," Myra said.

"It's okay Ma. Pa was there," Donald said. Linda watched as Myra's face changed once again, this time to hard and cold.

Obviously, Myra wasn't happy with her ex-husband being there. Forcing a smile, she said, "I guess it was about time he was there for something," then turned and walked into the kitchen.

A few minutes later, Myra returned carrying an apple pie and with a huge smile on her face. Her dark mood having changed yet again.

They sat at the table until late into the night, talking and laughing. Myra seemed to have fun telling Linda funny stories about her new husband.

The mood at the table changed again when Donald handed Myra a packet of papers.

"Ma, these are the forms. I just need them signed," Donald said.

Reaching for the packet, Myra asked, "You're sure this is what you want? You may get drafted anyway. Why don't you wait and see?"

"I've gotten several letters from Lewis and Manny. They both think this is the best thing for me, ma," Donald explained.

Lewis and Manny were Myra's older sons, both already in the Army. It struck Linda as odd Donald's brothers thought going in the Army was the best thing for him. Like her parents thinking getting married was the best thing for her.

"I don't care what Lewis and Manny think. I care about what you want," Myra said. "Are you sure? she asked.

"I'm sure, Ma. Please sign the papers," Donald pleaded.

"I'm curious," Myra asked, "why didn't you ask your father to sign these?"

Myra's questions were upsetting Donald. Linda watched his eyes harden when he answered, "I did."

"And what did he say?" Myra asked.

"Pa refused. He said since he hadn't been around to raise me, he felt it wasn't his place to say either way."

"Of course he did," Myra said, looking annoyed. "Look Donald, I'm worried. I know your brothers are encouraging you to join the Army, but I see the news. These are uncertain times. You know I'm an uneducated field worker, and all I ever wanted was for my sons was an education. I really wish you'd finish school first."

Cutting his mother off, Donald yelled saying, "An education? What kind of education could I possibly have gotten with all the moving around the last twelve years, Ma? I am failing all my classes and I'm probably not going to graduate, anyway."

Then, more sweetly, he added, "And I have a wife now to think about. This is my only choice. Lewis and Manny know it, too. Look Ma, it's late and we are all tired. Please, will you just sign the papers?" Donald asked.

Later in bed, with the papers signed giving parental permission for Donald to enter the Army, Linda whispered, "Donald, can I ask you a question?"

"I'm tired," Donald said. "Let's talk tomorrow."

"No, I have to know now," Linda said.

And without waiting for a reply, she asked, "Did you marry me just so your momma would sign those papers tonight?"

Turning over, Donald answered, "Don't be silly. I married you because I love you. Now go to sleep."

* * *

The next morning, they left Myra's and headed toward home.

Donald was leaving the following day for basic training and his mood was reflective, so he filled the return ride with stories of his brothers and his mother. Linda listened, feeling sorry for Donald as he told her about the day they sentenced his father to ten years in prison for involuntary manslaughter. He was only six years old. She saw the sadness in his eyes when he talked about only seeing his father on visiting days.

"When they released Pa a few months ago, I asked if I could live with him. Ma said yes, but only if I stayed in school and boy, am I glad I did," Donald said.

Confused, Linda asked, "Glad you did what?"

"Stayed to school, of course. If I hadn't, I wouldn't have met my beautiful wife," Donald answered.

Smiling, Linda said, "We met in church."

"Oh, that's right," Donald said, laughing and Linda laughed along.

Happy with the day, Linda asked, "Can I listen to the radio?" Again, not waiting for an answer, she turned it on. Finding a country music station, she sang along with every song, whether she knew the words or not.

In a small town outside of Fresno, they stopped at a motel for the night. Not wishing to be seen by anyone, Linda sat low in the seat while Donald checked them in. When he returned with the key, he said, "Guess what? They gave us the honeymoon suite."

"And just how did they know we were honeymooners?" Linda asked.

"Because they asked why I needed the room," Donald said.

"And what did you tell them?" Linda asked.

"I told them the truth. That we got married three days ago, and we're on a quick honeymoon before I leave for boot camp," he said. "I even had to show them our marriage certificate, so they'd believe me," Donald said as he pushed open the door of the Honeymoon Suite.

Linda walked in, turned on the light, and laughed. The honeymoon suite looked just like the room they stayed in two nights ago. The only difference was a larger bed and carpet on the floor.

"Oh, my goodness, there's carpet on the floor. I love carpet," Linda squealed. "I love the way it feels when I walk barefoot on it."

Laughing, Donald said, "Well, don't take your shoes off just yet. Let's go eat first."

The diner was just across the parking lot from the hotel, so after dinner they walked to the motel holding hands, sharing a cigarette.

There, Donald wooed Linda with his words, making her feel beautiful. They undressed slowly. Both shy and inexperienced, they gave each other free rein to look and to touch as they wished.

Unlike their wedding night, Donald was gentle and loving. Touching and kissing they allowed their excitement to grow until neither of them could wait a second longer.

He entered her slowly, and this time there was no pain.

They stayed awake late into the night, and in between their lovemaking, they smoked and talked, avoiding the subject of his leaving and their future. What was the point? Knowing he'd only be gone six weeks, Linda wasn't ready to think about living away from her momma and daddy yet. So instead, she allowed herself to get lost in the moment, thinking of nothing important until eventually they both drifted off to sleep.

* * *

It seemed like only minutes had passed when Donald woke her up.

"Honey, get up now. It's time to go," he whispered.

While Donald drove, Linda slept. When she woke again, it was to his kiss on her cheek. He said, "I'm going to miss you, but I promise to write every chance I get." Linda smiled up at him, saying nothing.

At the door, he kissed her sweetly on the lips and said, "I love you."

She watched until Donald's car was no longer in sight. Then she walked into the house, climbed the stairs, crawled into her bed, and was back to sleep in no time.

Hours later, when she woke up for the third time, her momma was in her room, sitting in what looked like a brand-new rocking chair, crocheting.

"Morning, Momma," Linda said, stretching. "What time is it?"

"It's after noon," her momma answered, rocking to-and-fro.

"You shoulda woke me," Linda said. "I would've gone to church with you."

"It's Monday, and there's no school, so I let you sleep," her momma said.

"Then was there somethin' you wanted?" Linda asked.

Looking up from her crocheting, her momma answered, saying, "Nah, I just came to check on you. Are you okay?" she asked.

Then Linda noticed the concern on her momma's face and wondered if she'd even slept a wink since she left.

"I'm fine, Momma," Linda said. "It was just like you said."

Picking up her crocheting, her momma said, "Good, now we'll wait and see if your time of the month comes."

Instantly sick to her stomach, she panicked thinking, *Dear God, what if I'm pregnant?* The possibility hadn't even occurred to her.

Flopping back on her pillow, Linda wondered what in the world she had thought was so romantic about being grown up.

Then she rolled over, hoping she could go back to sleep.

* * *

When her time of the month came, she literally prayed out loud, thanking God. It was bad enough being married at fifteen, but to be pregnant, too? She could just imagine what the kids at school were already saying.

If Linda knew anything at all, it was that she wasn't ready for a baby.

* * *

While Donald was gone, Linda received several letters from him. He told her basic training was harder than he thought it was going to be. And about "Sarge" constantly screaming at them, calling them scum bags and worse. He told her he'd made a new friend, Bob. And in each letter, he shared his hopes, dreams, and fears in deeply poetic words.

Mainly he told her how much he loved her, saying he knew he was going to marry her from the moment he'd seen her at school, which made Linda laugh. He said he remembered exactly what she wore; a blue shirt with a white collar and a black poodle skirt, neither of which she owned, still it melted her heart anyway.

She loved how open he was, wishing she'd met this Donald sooner. He wrote about his childhood, telling her how they'd moved from place to place following his father, who was moved from jail to jail whenever he got in trouble, which was often.

Linda felt like she learned more about Donald with each letter she received, and she looked forward to them. His letters always cheered her up somehow, giving her hope for the future. He wrote about his return, about their moving into their first home and having a family someday. Still uncertain about the family part, she looked forward to the day Donald would return and even wondered if maybe she was falling in love with her husband.

Lying across her bed, looking very much like the teenager she was, Linda opened the letter she received that day.

It began just like every other one. It read:

My Dearest Wife,

That was the only similarity to any of his other letters.

I can't believe boot camp is almost over. Graduation is next Wednesday, and I'll be flying home on Friday.
I'm sorry you can't be here for graduation, but I know you're finishing up with school.

She wondered what Donald was going to say when he found out she'd never gone back to school. Especially after the hard time she'd given him about dropping out. Linda couldn't face going back to school. It was bad enough at church, she knew everyone was just waiting to see if her belly was going to grow.

I'm guessing you must be busy since I haven't received even one letter from you.

No, she hadn't written back. She'd tried, but everything she wrote sounded stupid to her. Donald was good with words and Linda had no problem admitting she wasn't good at writing at all.

I am waiting for my orders now, telling me where we'll be stationed. I'm excited to start our life together and…

Linda laid the letter down on the bed. She couldn't read anymore, trying to hold back the tears that threatened to fall.

Of course, reading all of Donald's beautiful letters, full of hope and promise made it easy to think she was in love.

What had she been thinking? She wasn't ready to leave her momma and daddy. She didn't want a home of her own and wasn't ready to start a life with a stranger. Scared, and not knowing what else to do, Linda bowed her head and prayed.

"Dear God in Heaven," she begged, "you gotta help me. What do I do? I ain't ready for all this. I guess Momma was right when she said one day I'd be a wife, but I've got no idea how to be a wife. Dang it, she thought. I don't even like any of the things wives do."

Remembering the last time they made love, Linda blushed, thinking she did like that one.

Linda's prayer was interrupted when her momma walked in, saying, "Your daddy and I received a letter from Donald today. He says he'll be home on Friday and he plans to leave right away." There were tears in her momma's eyes when she said, "Linda, I know you're scared, but you need to be brave now. It will be an adjustment at first, but each day it'll get easier. You know your daddy and I were only a little older than you and Donald when we got married. We were just children, too. Anyway, my point is, we did fine and y'all will, too."

Without stopping to take a breath her momma went on saying, "Just think of it, soon you'll have a house of your own and one day you'll have babies and your daddy and I'll come visit all ya'll."

Not caring to hear anymore, Linda screamed, "Momma, stop!" She knew her momma was trying to make her feel better, but it wasn't helping. Right now, all she wanted was to run, to be outside running barefoot, playing hide-and-seek with her sister and brothers. Or to be down at the creek swimming with her cousins. To be anywhere else than where she was right now. Like it or not, though, she was married.

Changing the subject, Linda asked, "Momma, what are you fixin' for dinner?"

"Pork chops and collard greens. Why?" her momma answered.

"Because my husband's comin' home Friday and I can't cook a thing. I think it's about time I learned to cook somethin'," she answered.

Leaving Home

Leaving her momma and daddy was the hardest thing Linda had ever done. Donald received orders for Fort Irwin Army Base in Barstow, only three hours from her parents, but to Linda, it may as well have been halfway around the world. They arrived at their military issued duplex full of military issued everything with nothing except the clothes in their suitcases.

Linda took stock of her new home. The living room furniture consisted of an uncomfortable looking green couch with a matching chair. The highlight of the room was the small black and white television in a corner. To her left was a small dining area.

In the kitchen, a stove and refrigerator were separated by a large sink. And against the wall was a small table for two. There were two bedrooms, each with a bed, a nightstand, and a dresser. In between the bedrooms was a small bathroom.

Setting their suitcases down in the first bedroom, Donald kissed Linda on the cheek, saying, "I've got to report in. I'll see you later."

Not knowing exactly what to do, she unpacked her few belongings, then sat down on the back porch smoking cigarette after cigarette, waiting for Donald to return.

Remembering the phone on the kitchen wall, Linda dialed her momma's number. Feeling silly, she hung up when her momma answered. After all, she'd only been gone a few hours.

* * *

Linda and Donald fell quickly into a routine of sorts. Each morning while Donald ate breakfast, Linda packed his lunch. When he finished eating, he'd give her a peck on her cheek and before he walked out the door, he'd say with a wink, "Behave yourself." Pretending to be amused, Linda laughed at his joke.

At night, Donald came home, again kissing her on the cheek, pretending to love whatever she cooked for dinner. She knew he was pretending because she hated her own cooking, but thought it sweet of him to lie. Her crash course in cooking had obviously taught her nothing because soon Donald started taking her out to dinner at the NCO club, saying he was giving her a break. Another good lie.

He'd come home and say, "Let's go for a ride," which meant, "let's go get burgers and fries."

* * *

After receiving her morning peck and admonishment to "behave," Linda watched Donald drive away. Grabbing a piece of burnt bacon, she picked up the phone, and dialed her momma's number.

The phone rang twice before her momma answered, giving her just enough time to finish chewing.

Smiling cheerfully, Linda said, "Hi, Momma."

"Is everything okay?" her momma asked.

"Yeah, why?" Linda asked. "Don't I sound okay?"

"Yes, you sound fine, but we just talked two days ago," her momma said, laughing. "So, I thought maybe somethin' was wrong."

"No, nothing's wrong. I'm just bored, Momma," Linda sighed.

"That's cause you need to find things to do. Like cleanin' and doin' the washin'," her momma scolded.

"Boring," Linda said, rolling her eyes. She realized housework didn't suit her. And she despised doing the wash. Lying, Linda said, "I've already done em', Momma."

"Then you can prepare for supper," her momma said, obviously frustrated.

"I ain't even cleaned up from breakfast yet, and I ain't got no idea what I'm makin' for supper," Linda moaned.

"Then I suggest you get pregnant. A baby'll help. Then you'll be too busy to be bored," her momma said.

Deflated, Linda hung up the phone.

As far as marriages went, the only point of reference Linda had was her parents' and she wasn't sure they were a good gauge. You could say her childhood was difficult. Since her daddy worked in the fields, when he finished a job, most times they'd move on to the next job. Other times he'd get fired or quit and they'd pack up what little they had and hit the road. To Linda, those were the best times.

All of them piled into the car—where they were heading, no one knew. Nothing seemed boring then. Everything was new and exciting, and Linda was happiest when they were in the car, singing to the radio. And when they weren't singing, Linda could spend hours looking out the window, daydreaming or counting the cows in the fields.

Sometimes weeks went by before her daddy found work, and they'd sleep in the car or on a riverbank where they ate whatever fish they caught. It may have been hard times but it certainly wasn't boring.

Because they moved around so much, there was very little traditional schooling. Insisting they were not going to be stupid, though, her daddy made them practice their letters and numbers while he drove. They'd started off in Arkansas and finally settled in California.

Realizing she was smiling, remembering these as her happiest times, Linda wondered what it was going to take to make her happy now. And while her momma was usually right about most things, she knew having a baby was not what she needed.

After days of pondering the subject, Linda knew exactly what would make her happy. It was to go home and visit her parents. Alone. She didn't want Donald to take her, and she didn't need him to either because she already knew how to drive. Her daddy taught her and her siblings how to drive. Sometimes when he was tired, he'd pull over and let one of them drive. Usually, it was one of her brothers, but sometimes he'd let Linda drive, and she loved it. She felt free behind the wheel.

Yes, Linda knew exactly what she needed. A car. And, of course, a driver's license.

* * *

A few weeks later, with a plan in place of how to convince Donald she needed a car and a driver's license, Linda made spaghetti with meat and tomato sauce for dinner. So far, it was the second meal she'd mastered, and it seemed to be Donald's favorite.

Knowing he liked it when she dressed up, she took special care as she put on her best dress. She ran a comb through her hair and added a touch of lipstick. Looking in the mirror, Linda surveyed herself.

Her hair was shoulder length and the same color as her eyes, mousy brown. And although she wasn't a raving beauty, her daddy always told her that her smile could light up any room.

Linda intended to use her best smile tonight. She not only wanted to wow Donald, she wanted him eating out of her hands.

The spaghetti was done, the bread was ready to go into the oven. Having made a fresh batch of sun tea, she had a glass poured and waiting for Donald.

Walking through the front door, Donald said, "Wow, something smells good."

From the kitchen, Linda yelled. "I made your favorite. Sit down. It's about ready."

Within minutes, Linda carried Donald's plate into the dining room and his reaction was perfect. She watched as his eyes lit up, taking it all in.

"How was your day, dear?" she asked.

If he answered, Linda didn't hear it. Picking up his green jacket, she walked to the closet and hung it up. Facing the wall, she paused, closed her eyes, took a deep breath, ready to give the performance of a lifetime. As she turned back around, she gave Donald her biggest smile and said, "Come on, sit-down, let's eat. I'm starvin'."

In what seemed like five minutes, Donald had finished eating and was ready to move to the living room, where Linda knew he'd turn on the television and she'd lose her chance.

As Donald rose to leave the table, a panicked Linda yelled, "Donald, wait a minute, I got somethin' to talk to you about."

Looking concerned, he sat back down and asked, "Is everything okay?"

"Yes, fine, but I've been thinking," Linda said as she lit a cigarette.

Amused, Donald asked, "Really? What have you been thinking about?"

Linda knew if she waited too long, she'd lose what little courage she had, so she blurted it out, "I wanna get my driver's license and I want you to buy me a car." Continuing, she pointed out all the things she could get done in a day, the banking, the shopping, and picking up his uniforms from the cleaners.

"Those are all the things we do together on the weekend," Donald argued.

"And I will miss doing them together," Linda said, "but if I do them during the week, we'd have more time to do other things on the weekends."

When Donald didn't appear convinced, a frustrated Linda moved on to Plan B.

Seductively, she grabbed his hand, looked up and, in her sexist voice said, "Then if I can't convince you by talkin', how about I show you one thing we'd have more time to do, if I had a car?"

The night of lovemaking did the trick. Donald agreed Linda should have a car. The following week, Donald took her to get her driver's license, and he bought her a car. It was a Ford somethin' or other, but Linda couldn't care less what kind of car it was. As long as it had four wheels and worked, she was thrilled.

The car had done wonders for her disposition. Every day after Donald left, Linda hurried to get her housework done. Then she'd head out, the country radio station blasting, going anywhere she could get away with, singing.

* * *

It had only been six months since Linda left, but arriving home, she found nothing as she remembered it.

William was nowhere to be found and when she asked where he was, she was told he was rarely home, choosing to spend most of his time at his girlfriend's house.

"Where's Daddy?" Linda asked.

"Your daddy is at the bar and he's probably had a few too many. I'll just run up there and get him. You stay with Arnie," her momma said. "I'll be right back."

When they returned home hours later, it was obvious they'd both had a few too many. To Linda, her daddy looked older and tired. Her momma, withdrawn. And the entire time she was there, her brother Arnie stayed in his bedroom.

She left feeling sad. Maybe it was because she had some slight experience with marriage now, but Linda was thinking her parents had been better off on the road. The years "settled" seem to cause discontent in them both.

* * *

Donald and Linda had been married for almost a year when Donald again mentioned the subject of a baby. By that time, the excitement of her car had faded. The life she remembered with her momma and daddy was gone forever, so Linda conceded that the next logical thing to do was to start a family.

* * *

A year later, Linda still wasn't pregnant. Her momma and her few female friends assured her she had nothing to worry about, though, so Linda put the situation in God's hands. Just the simple act of prayer helped her greatly, but it did nothing for Donald. For Donald, there seemed to be an urgency for her to get pregnant and he insisted she go see a doctor.

To which Linda argued, saying, "I ain't goin' to see no doctor. I told you I put it in God's hands. If we are supposed to have a baby, we will."

"Damn it Linda," Donald yelled, "I need you to get pregnant now."

"Excuse me," Linda said, "I don't understand. Please explain what you mean when you say you need me to get pregnant now?"

"It just means I am afraid there may be something wrong," Donald explained.

"Would it make a difference if there was?" Linda asked. "What if I can't get pregnant? What then?"

"Don't even think such a thing. You will get pregnant," Donald yelled.

"Okay, but I'm telling you there ain't nothing wrong with me and I ain't goin' to see no doctor," Linda yelled back at him, storming out of the room.

Lying in the dark, Linda wondered if Donald's desperation for her to get pregnant had something to do with the fact the war in Vietnam was escalating and he might not be home much longer.

* * *

Two months later, still not pregnant, discouraged, Linda agreed to see the doctor. On the day of her appointment, she'd begged to go alone, but Donald insisted on going with her.

Sitting in the waiting room, just prior to being called in to see the doctor, Donald whispered, "Listen, you need to let me do all the talking." A few minutes later, she sat across from the doctor, with her head down like a naughty child, as Donald expressed his opinion of their problem. Linda didn't agree, but as instructed, she let Donald do all the talking.

The doctor, who appeared to be listening intently to Donald, said, "Mr. Holloway, I doubt there's anything wrong. However, if Mrs. Holloway agrees, I can examine her."

Linda had only seen a doctor a few times in her life and never a gynecologist, but for everyone's sake, she agreed.

The nurse escorted her into an adjacent room and handed her a white paper gown.

"You'll need to undress. Put the gown on with the…" Linda didn't hear the rest. Her hands were shaking uncontrollably, and she felt like she was going to be sick.

"Mrs. Holloway, did you hear me, honey?" the nurse asked.

With tears threatening to fall, and her heart beating so hard she was sure it was going to explode, Linda said, "Please call me Linda. And I'm sorry ma'am, I'm just scared. See, I ain't seen many doctors in my life and never a lady's one."

"Mrs. Holloway," the nurse said, then corrected herself, "I'm sorry, Linda, you don't need to worry," the nurse assured her with a little squeeze on her arm. "I'll be here the whole time."

After the nurse left, Linda did as she was told. She undressed, put on the gown with the opening facing the back, got up on the table and laid back. Overcome with emotion, Linda rolled over, pulled her legs up to her chest, and cried.

Walking in with his nurse accompanied him, the doctor said, "Okay, Mrs. Holloway, I need you to slide down on the table," oblivious to her tears.

With the nurse's help, Linda did as she was told.

When the doctor finished his exam, he took off his gloves, threw them in the garbage, and walked out without saying a word.

The nurse helped her sit up, asking, "Are you okay?"

"Yes, I'm fine. Thank you for being so kind," Linda answered.

Back in the doctor's office, they were told everything appeared to be fine. ",You go on home and don't worry," the doctor assured them, "you'll get pregnant in time. However," he added, "Mr. Holloway, if your wife isn't pregnant in six months, I suggest you get checked. The problem could be with you."

* * *

The love making, the monthly let downs, and the constant fighting were exhausting. Becoming more obsessed, Donald accused Linda of being reluctant.

"Reluctant? What in the hell does that even mean?" Linda asked.

"Reluctant means I don't think you want to get pregnant," Donald answered.

"Oh, believe me, Donald, I wanna be pregnant just as much as you want me to. No," she said, correcting herself, "I want it even more than you 'cause, if I was pregnant, then maybe you'd leave me the hell alone."

Nightly they tried. And nightly, afterwards, Linda curled up in a ball with tears streaming down her face, unable to sleep, wondering why God was punishing her.

Other nights, the exhaustion won, and she'd sleep blissfully lost in her dreams. Her dreams were mostly of riding in the backseat of her daddy's station wagon, singing her heart out with her brothers and sisters. Oh, how they loved to sing. All four of them cramped up together in the back seat, Mabel and Linda screaming, each trying to outdo the other, but none of them could carry a tune in a bucket. Except Linda.

Her moods fluctuated, too. Disappointed in herself, at eighteen-years-old she'd been married for almost three years and still couldn't cook a decent meal. She hated cleaning the house and her house reflected it. Looking around, it took little to convince her she'd failed at everything. Even getting pregnant.

Most days, not knowing what else to do, she'd get in her car and tune the radio to the country station. Turning it up, she'd drive for hours, singing.

* * *

Several more months had passed when Linda made another appointment to see the doctor, this time without telling Donald. The doctor assured her once again saying, "Mrs. Holloway, there was nothing physically wrong with you. I think you're trying too hard. I have a suggestion," he said, "if you care to hear it."

"Yes please, I'm willing to try almost anything," Linda answered.

With a big smile and a wink, the doctor said, "I want you to get dressed up and go out. Go to a party, have a few drinks, and relax. Then when you get home," he said, "I want you to let nature takes its course."

Walking out of the exam room thinking the appointment had been a huge waste of her time, the doctor's nurse handed her a piece of paper saying, "Linda, the doctor asked me to give you this."

Hesitating, Linda asked, "What is this?"

"It's a prescription," the nurse answered. "The doctor thinks it'll help you relax."

She took the prescription and put it in her purse, now convinced the visit had been a waste of time. Was her doctor really suggesting she needed both drugs and alcohol to get pregnant?

Nervous, but also curious about what Donald was going to think of the doctor's suggestion, Linda confessed she'd been back to see the doctor.

"Really? What did he say?" Donald asked.

"He says we're trying too hard and suggests we get dressed up and go out. He says we should drink and relax," she answered.

Throwing his head back and laughing, Donald asked, "He says we're trying too hard, huh?"

"Yes, that's what he said," she answered. "I swear it."

"And the doctor thinks a pretty dress and a bottle of booze will help?" Donald asked.

"That's what he said," Linda answered.

She handed Donald the prescription, adding, "He even suggested I take these pills to help relax me."

Linda was on the verge of tears when Donald said, "Well then, if it is doctor's orders, that's exactly what we're going to do."

They spent the rest of the evening making plans. With New Year's Eve not far off, Donald suggested they go to dinner and then dancing at the club on base.

Linda agreed it sounded like fun.

They'd just climbed into bed and Donald was about to turn out the light when Linda said, "Donald, I have a request."

Lovingly stroking her arm, Donald said, "I'm listening?"

Holding her breath, unsure of the reaction she might get, Linda said, "I don't wanna make love again until New Year's Eve."

And to her amazement, Donald not only agreed, but said, "And I think you should go out and buy a new dress for the occasion, too."

"Seriously, that's not necessary," Linda said. "Thank you anyway."

"No, I insist," Donald said, "and make it something extra pretty."

So, with a new dress hanging in the closet, a well-rested Linda looked forward to New Year's Eve.

Each day, Linda took the medication the doctor prescribed. She felt lighter, happier somehow, and looked at each new day as a gift. She got up each morning and made Donald's breakfast. She accepted his peck on the cheek before he left and laughed at his admonishment to behave. She cleaned the house with new enthusiasm and looking forward to his return.

Since lovemaking was off the table, they spent their evenings watching television or playing cards.

Enthralled in their newfound happiness, both seemingly had forgotten what the purpose of the night was.

New Year's Eve was on a Saturday and since they'd be out late, they slept in. Waking slowly, Donald and Linda lay in bed talking softly and laughing happily at each other's jokes when suddenly, Donald jumped up, saying, "I'm hungry, woman. I think I'll make breakfast today. Are you hungry?" he asked.

Smiling at Donald's playfulness, Linda answered, "No! I'm starving."

While she waited for breakfast, a comfy and contented Linda fell back to sleep and was in a pleasant dream when Donald woke her up.

He was holding a tray full of perfectly cooked eggs, bacon, and toast in one hand. His other hand was behind his back and his guilty smile was enough to make Linda ask, "What are you hiding behind your back, dear?"

When Donald produced a very expensive-looking bottle of champagne, Linda gasped.

"Where'd you get somethin' like that?" she asked.

"Does it matter?" he asked.

Smiling, reaching for a piece of toast, Linda answered, "Not really."

They sat in bed eating, talking, and drinking happily, and before either of them knew it, the bottle was empty. Drunk, naked, and happy, they made love into the early afternoon. And as the time drew nearer to their appointed dinner time, neither of them wanted to move.

Finally, Donald said, "It's getting late. I think we need to get ready for dinner," devilishly adding, "and to save time, I think we should shower together."

Acting shocked but loving the idea, Linda asked, "What? Are you serious?"

"Very serious," he said, pulling her off the bed.

In the shower, they washed each other's bodies, blushing like virgins when their soapy hands touched private places.

Later, wrapped in each other's arms, neither thinking about the past nor the future, they lay content in the present. And never made it to dinner.

Gina

By late February, Linda was sure she was pregnant but, wanting it confirmed before she told Donald, she made a doctor's appointment.

Reaching out his hand, the doctor said, "Hello Mrs. Holloway. What can I do for you today?"

"I'm late," she answered, smiling nervously.

"Wonderful," he said, smiling ear to ear.

After a quick examination, the doctor confirmed Linda was two months pregnant. Teasing her, he said, "So, I guess your night out must have done the trick?"

Linda blushed slightly remembering the events and said, "I guess so."

After she told Donald she was pregnant, beyond excited, he treated Linda like a princess, expecting nothing of her, and she wanted for nothing.

While they waited for the arrival of their baby, they kept busy. Donald celebrated his fourth year in the Army, which earned him additional leave, so they took a road trip. First, seeing Linda's family, then driving north to see Donald's family.

They painted the second bedroom, christening it the nursery, and bought a secondhand crib and a dresser.

The months of her pregnancy flew by quickly and, as the end neared, Linda felt happy, rested, and content, having enjoyed the best months of their marriage. And though he hadn't said as much, Linda knew the smile on Donald's face meant he felt it, too.

Feeling tired in her ninth month Linda slowed down, but maintained a joy that bubbled up every time she felt her baby kick. Donald took time off from work and together they waited, sitting in front of the television eating pot pies.

* * *

Linda had just fallen asleep when she woke up wet. Embarrassed, she said, "Donald, wake up! I think I just wet the bed."

"What?" he asked sleepily. "Are you sure?"

"Yes," was all she could manage before a contraction hit. Drawing her knees up to her chin, Linda grabbed her belly and instinctively panted until it passed. "Or maybe my water just broke."

When the contraction passed, Linda got up, changed her clothes, stripped the bed, then sat down calmly on the edge of the bed.

Looking pale, Donald asked, "Are you okay?"

Linda felt sorry for him but had no time to console him as another contraction hit. This time, watching Donald bend over as if he was having the contraction caused Linda to laugh.

"You look terrible. Why don't you go wait in the living room," Linda said.

"Aren't you ready to go?" he asked.

"No, I promised momma I'd call her when the time came," Linda said.

Assuring Donald there was time Linda dialed her momma's number.

When she heard her momma's voice, Linda, crying like a five-year-old, said, "Momma."

"Linda, is that you?" her momma asked. "Oh Lord, it's the baby, isn't it? Oh my, I wish I could be there."

"Yes Momma, it's me," Linda whispered. "My water just broke, and it hurts bad."

"Is Donald there with you?" her momma asked.

"Yes, he is right here," she said as the third contraction hit.

Linda felt the blood drain from her face. She felt sick. Scared to death, she whispered, "I wish you were too, Momma."

"I think we should go now," Donald whispered.

Linda nodded her head, agreeing. "Hey Momma, I gotta go," Linda said, doubling over again. "We're going to the hospital now. I'll have Donald call you later."

They arrived at the hospital as the baby's head was crowning, and they rushed Linda into the delivery room. Her labor and delivery happened so fast there wasn't any time for preparations.

Thirty minutes later, Linda cried as they placed a tiny red wiggly baby girl, crying at the top of her lungs, into her arms.

Much later settled in her room, exhausted but happy, Linda watched as Donald held his daughter, gently rocking her back and forth.

"What should we name her?" he asked.

"I was thinkin' Gina Marie," Linda answered, "after my great grandma."

Looking down at their sleeping baby girl, Donald whispered, "Gina Marie Holloway, welcome to the world."

* * *

Two days later, they brought Gina home. She weighed just over five pounds. Donald stayed home for a few days, but before Linda felt ready, he went back to work, leaving her to handle their tiny daughter alone.

She worried constantly because mothering didn't seem to come naturally for her and, from the beginning everything that could go wrong, did. First, Linda's milk didn't come in and sure Gina was going to starve to death, she nursed until she bled. When the frustrated Gina cried, Linda cried, too. Then, exhausted, they'd both sleep. Until Gina, hungry again, was awake and crying.

At her wit's end, Linda called her doctor, and was delighted when he suggested putting Gina on formula. "This will help until your milk comes in," he assured her.

Then there were the rest of the chores, which now were solely her responsibility. She spent her days feeding Gina, cleaning, and trying to keep up with the washing, all the while waiting for Donald to get home, hoping for some help.

With the birth of their baby behind them, Donald seemed to have lost interest in both wife and baby. He seemed distracted and was little to no help. With each passing day, Linda grew more and more tired. There were days she was too tired to even carry Gina to the nursery after her feedings. Concerned she might roll over on her in the bed, though, Linda made a makeshift cradle out of the bottom drawer of her dresser. She set it on the floor next to the bed so when Gina slept, Linda could, too.

Falling further behind in her chores and realizing motherhood was overwhelming her, she struggled to find her way until, in frustration, she finally went to Donald, begging for help.

"Donald, I need help," Linda said.

"You don't need help. You need a plan," Donald said. "I did all the housekeeping and worked while you were pregnant with Gina. It's easy. You just need to get into a routine. When Gina sleeps, you do whatever needs to be done. It's simple."

"My momma has offered to come help, and I'd love to see her," Linda said. "Please, can my momma come? Just for a short visit?"

"No, absolutely not. We don't need help. We're just fine here," Donald shouted.

At his refusal, anger welled up inside her and Linda yelled, "You may be fine, Donald, but I ain't. I need some help and I need some sleep. So, if Momma can't come help me, then you're gonna have to."

"Listen Linda," Donald said, "I hesitated to tell you this, but I think you need to know. Things are heating up in Vietnam and there is more and more talk about our unit being deployed. We've been preparing and sending caravans of trucks, tanks, and artillery south on carriers. We are just waiting for the call for more troops to man them. It appears the Viet Cong are gaining ground. The South Vietnamese are asking for more help and our generals are telling us it looks like the President will be forced to send in more ground troops. So, it appears the US will join this war sooner than later."

Linda wondered why he was telling her this now. How was hearing she may be left here alone with Gina going to help?

"Do you really think they'll send you to Vietnam?" she asked. "We just had a baby. Certainly they'd take that into consideration."

"You've always known I'd probably be going to Vietnam," he reminded her. "So yes, it's really just a matter of when. And since I'm sure I'm not the only soldier who just became a father, I doubt they'll make an exception for me," he said sarcastically.

What will happen to Gina and me if you don't come back? was what she wanted to ask, but didn't.

Despite the warmth of the day, Linda sat shivering, with tears running down her face. She didn't want to think of war or its implications right now. She just wanted help.

"Listen, Donald said, why don't you go make a bottle for Gina, then you can lie down. I'm not going to bed for a while. If she's still awake when I'm ready for bed, I'll wake you up. Now go on. You don't need your momma. I'm here and I promise I'll try to help more."

Not sure she believed him but too tired to argue, Linda changed Gina's diaper, made her a bottle, and left her in Donald's arms. Numb and tired, she crawled into bed, pulled the covers over her head, and cried herself to sleep.

* * *

Three months later, granted a brief vacation, Donald took her to stay with her momma and daddy's while he went fishing with his father for a few days. He'd been true to his word and helped her as much as he could, and Linda was happy he was getting to spend time with his father, too.

During her stay, she and Gina slept in her old bedroom. With familiar surroundings and with her momma's help, she slept better than she had in a long time. Her siblings, both near and far, came to visit with their families. Sitting around the table, they reminisced about the places they'd traveled, laughing at the antics one or all of them had gotten in to over the years. Even her momma and daddy looked happy again, and it thrilled Linda to see there was no alcohol in the house.

With Gina asleep upstairs, Linda volunteered to help her momma clean up after dinner. "I'll wash if you dry, Momma," Linda said.

"You got a deal," her momma said, smiling.

Lost in thought, Linda washed while her momma dried. "Momma, can I ask you a question?"

"Of course," her momma answered.

"Have you ever felt like you were a failure?" she asked.

"Yeah sure, sometimes. I think it's normal. I'm sure everybody probably feels like a failure at some point. However, you, my dear girl, ain't been alive long enough to have failed at anything."

Linda smiled, knowing that wasn't true. She felt as if she'd failed at everything. She'd failed herself mostly for not standing up for herself, and not following her dreams.

With tears in her eyes, Linda admitted, "I don't know how to take care of Gina."

Frustrated and sounding angrier than she really felt, Linda said, "And you were wrong, Momma, havin' a baby hasn't helped a thing.

In fact, it made it worse. The house is a mess. I'm tired all the time. And Donald and I barely speak."

"This too will pass, dear," was all her momma had to say.

Speechless, Linda rinsed the last dish just as her sister Mabel walked in. Handing Linda a crying baby, she said, "I think someone wants you."

Looking first at Linda, then at her momma, Mabel asked, "Are you two okay?"

"Just fine," Linda said, taking Gina from Mabel, excusing herself.

* * *

The next day, Linda sat in her momma's high back rocking chair feeding Gina, thinking about the dream she had the night before.

She dreamed Donald left to go fishing and didn't come back for them. As she sat rocking back and forth, she allowed the scenario to play out in her head; abandoned here with Gina at her parents, never seeing Donald or her army issued home again, then waited to see if she was going to feel some kind of emotion. Any trace of emotion. Would she be happier if he didn't come back? And would she be happy to see him if he did?

The following day, Donald returned and Linda got her answer. Just the sound of his voice downstairs caused her melancholy to return.

As she packed their things to leave, Linda said a silent prayer, hoping her momma was right and this, whatever it was, would pass.

* * *

Sadly, nothing passed except time. She and Donald grew further and further apart. The news of Donald's impending deployment to Vietnam had made matters worse and came with a whole new set of worries for Linda. What was going to happen to her and Gina when Donald went to Vietnam? Where would they live? How would they get by?

And what if he didn't come back? Linda wasn't that naïve. She knew he may not come back from Vietnam at all, and that only added to her anxiety.

As the memory of her visit home faded further and further away, Linda sunk deeper and deeper into what she now called her sadness.

Although she dreaded the daytime when Donald was gone, leaving her alone with Gina, she dreaded the nighttime more when he was home because, though he barely spoke to her during the day, at night, he still tried to engage her in sex.

Linda wanted nothing to do with sex, but lacking the strength to fight him, she lay there, allowing him to do what was necessary. Never satisfied though, Donald started belittling her.

"Seriously," Donald said, rolling off her, "was that the best you could do? I'd get more pleasure out of sex with my pillow."

Walking toward the bathroom door, Linda yelled, "Then please be my guest."

Slamming the door behind her, she bent over the toilet and vomited. Realizing her period was late, knowing the last thing she needed was to get pregnant again, Linda made a mental note to call the doctor and ask about some sort of birth control.

Relieved when her time of the month came a few days later, she never called the doctor.

* * *

By the time Gina was six months old, she was sleeping less during the day and more at night, but still when Gina napped, so did Linda. There were times, so tired, she'd put Gina in her crib to play while she slept.

Donald had come home unexpectedly several times to find Gina in her crib, soaking wet, crying, and Linda sound asleep. It seemed no matter how much she slept, she was still always tired.

No matter how much she wanted to be good at mothering, Linda knew she wasn't cut out for the job. Every day she longed to be anywhere besides this godforsaken Army base with Donald and a baby who exhausted her. She went through the motions, sad, lonely, and sleepy. With no one to talk to except Gina, Linda withdrew more and more.

During Gina's six-month checkup, the pediatrician made the mistake of asking Linda how she was doing, and she burst into tears, unloading on the poor man.

He listened quietly until she stopped talking, then looked at her with such compassion and understanding that Linda could've kissed him.

"I'm sorry, Doctor," Linda said. "Truly I am, but I feel like I can't take much more. And I don't know how to explain it. There's just this sadness, and I'm sleepy all the time."

"Mrs. Holloway, don't you have someone you can talk to?" he asked

"I've tried to talk to my husband," she said, "but he won't listen. He says I just need a routine and I'll be fine."

"Then what about your mother?" the doctor suggested.

Thinking about the numerous times she'd talked to her momma, Linda said, "I've tried talkin' to my momma. She says it's normal and it'll pass."

"Mrs. Holloway, your mother could be right," the pediatrician said, "but, in the meantime, I think you need to talk to someone. Someone professional."

Linda left, promising to call her doctor right away for a referral to a therapist. The thought of talking to anyone sounded exhausting, so she decided to try talking to her momma again.

After putting Gina down for a nap, she lit a cigarette and dialed her momma's number. Hearing her voice and crying uncontrollably, Linda said, "Momma, I'm scared. Somethin' ain't right with me,"

"What's the matter now?" her momma asked.

"I'm just so tired," Linda said. "I don't wanna to take care of Gina, this house, or Donald. And now I'm startin' to cry all the time."

"Linda, I told you this is all normal. I promise you're gonna be fine. Your baby is only six months old. You gotta give it time," her momma said.

She knew she sounded like a whiny child, but Linda didn't care. "Even Gina's doctor is concerned and thinks I need to talk to someone."

"Linda Lee, I'm only gonna say this once. That Doctor ain't got any idea what you're going through, but I do. And I assure you, this is normal. You just gotta let them hormones run their course, you'll see."

Then, in a sweeter voice, her momma said, "And you say you're tired. Well, of course you are, babies need lots of care. As Gina gets older, it'll get better. You'll see. I promise you there ain't nothin' wrong with you."

Linda hung up in utter despair. Her momma may think she was fine, but deep-down Linda knew something wasn't right. She wasn't fine.

She considered calling Mabel, but figured she'd probably just tell her the same thing. So Linda did nothing, and each day she got worse.

She stopped smiling. She didn't leave the house unless it was necessary. Even the idea of getting dressed to go out was daunting. So, if she had to leave the house, she'd put a large coat over her pajamas, slip on her shoes and go.

Helpless to do anything else, Linda waited for the magical day her momma promised. The day she'd wake up and feel like herself again.

* * *

That day still hadn't come when the fancy invitation arrived in the mail. It was an invitation to a wedding reception for Donald's brother Lewis and his wife Kaitlyn.

Linda vaguely remembered Donald telling her something about his brother Lewis coming home from Europe and getting married. And, of course, Donald was thrilled.

"It's been three years since I've seen my brother. And all the family will be there. Besides," he said, "you need to get out of this house and it's time for my family to meet Gina."

"No Donald, I don't wanna go. You go. I'll stay here with the baby," Linda said.

She could tell by the look on Donald's face he wasn't happy with her, but desperately, Linda pleaded, "I'm serious Donald, you go. Gina and I'll be fine here alone."

Raising his voice. Donald said, "I'm not going to a family function alone. My brothers want to meet you, and Ma is begging to see Gina. What would I tell them?"

"I don't know, but you better think of somethin'," Linda said. "Because I ain't going."

They argued for days, and in the end Linda gave in and agreed to go.

* * *

It was already late when they arrived at Myra's house. Linda was tired and longed to go straight to bed, but the entire family was there and obviously in a pre-party mood.

Gina, who slept the entire five-hour drive, was now wide awake and the center of attention.

Interrupting his conversation with his brother, Linda whispered, "Donald, do you think anyone would care if I went to bed?"

"I would," Donald whispered back. "Damn it, Linda, can't you at least try to have some fun?" Then he turned his back to her, returning to his conversation.

Feeling slighted but not wanting to make a scene, Linda turned back to the conversation on the other side of the room.

"How old is your baby?" Kaitlyn asked.

Trying her best to muster up a smile for her new sister-in-law, Linda answered, "She just turned seven months."

"She's beautiful. Congratulations," Kaitlyn said.

Trying to hide a yawn, Linda thanked her.

Just as Linda's family had, Donald's family fell instantly in love with Gina. Her aunts took turns holding and feeding her. When Grandma Myra insisted on bathing her, Linda didn't object.

In fact, the first two days, she barely got out of bed. From her bed upstairs, she could hear Donald trying to make excuses for her.

When she heard Myra scold Donald, saying, "New mothers need all the rest they can get, let her sleep," Linda had a whole new love and appreciation for her mother-in-law. Smiling, she drifted back to sleep, thinking finally someone understood.

Awaking, Linda lay with her eyes opened, listening to the sound of Donald's family gathered around the table downstairs, laughing and joking. Remembering the time not that long ago when she'd been laughing and joking with her own family, she couldn't help feeling a little envious.

A few minutes later, hearing Donald's footsteps in the hall, Linda closed her eyes and pretended to be sleeping.

Shaking her gently, Donald said, "Linda, honey, it's time to wake up now. I got good news. Ma has agreed to watch Gina while we go out for a bit. I was thinking we'd go to dinner and afterward take a drive. You could listen to country music on the radio." Tenderly adding, "All the things you love."

Never opening her eyes, Linda said, "Not tonight, maybe tomorrow." She could feel Donald stiffen as he said coolly, "We have a sitter tonight. So, you need to get up now and get in the bath."

Linda knew if she could hear them downstairs they would hear them fighting, so she got up, dressed, combed her hair, and put on lipstick.

Standing at the bottom of the stairs, in a faded blue dress, Linda saw Gina sleeping in her Aunt Kaitlyn's arms, peaceful and content. Looking up from Gina's face to Kaitlyn's, Linda's eyes rested upon her sister-in-law. She was beautiful beyond words. From the moment she'd met Kaitlyn, Linda felt self-conscious. And now, watching Kaitlyn with Gina, she felt a deep resentment. Kaitlyn made it look so easy sitting poised and relaxed, holding Gina.

After a slight buzz around them, she and Donald left on their date.

"Dear God, with all the fuss they made, you'd think we were goin' to our high school prom instead of just out to dinner while our infant daughter slept in the arms of her near perfect auntie," Linda said.

Looking over at her, Donald smiled but said nothing.

They went to the local diner, where they ate in silence. After dinner, again in silence, they drove to a nearby park where Donald parked the car and said, "Okay, I'm listening. Talk to me, Linda."

Linda just sat staring at Donald. What in the hell could she possibly say to him she hadn't already said? How was she supposed to explain what she didn't understand herself?

"I've got nothing to say. Can we go home now?" Linda asked.

Refusing her request, Donald pointed out that she had a baby now and a husband who loved her, and that alone should make her happy.

Donald was right and Linda knew it. She knew she should be happy, but she wasn't. And all the things Donald said ought to be making her happy were all the things Linda was sure were doing the exact opposite.

In a crazed state, Linda opened the car door and got out, slamming the door and took off running, wanting to be as far away from Donald as she could get. If she could have, Linda might've kept running.

Tired, she fell to the ground, crying. When no more tears came, she just laid there on the hard, cold ground.

Approaching her, Donald bent down consoling her lovingly. Cringing, Linda pulled away from him and screamed, "Don't you touch me!"

"Linda, please take my hand. Let me help you up," Donald begged.

Looking up, she saw a sad-faced Donald with his hand outstretched and almost felt sorry for him. Refusing his help, she got up, drying her eyes as she walked back to the car.

She was sitting in the driver's seat smoking a cigarette when Donald walked up.

"Look Linda, we need to talk," Donald said.

"I know we do," Linda snapped back at him. "And you're right, I should be happy and countin' my blessings, but I ain't. I wanna be happy, really, I do, Donald. I just can't pretend to be something I ain't."

Then, speaking from her heart, Linda added, "I ain't been a good wife to you or a good momma to Gina. The truth is, I never wanted to be either one. I married you 'cause my momma said to. And when I wasn't happy after we got married, she said it was 'cause I needed a baby. Momma was wrong. I look at my baby and I feel no joy. She's a burden to me," Linda said, crying again.

Feeling brave, Linda went on asking, "Do you wanna know why I sleep all the time, Donald? It's 'cause asleep I can forget I'm a wife and have a baby. When I sleep, you and Gina don't exist, and I don't hate you or me. When I'm asleep, I am happy!"

Determined to speak the truth no matter how much it hurt either of them, she continued without taking a breath, "And there ain't a day that goes by I don't feel worthless and ashamed of myself for it. Please Donald, I'm tired. Can we go home now?" she asked.

Neither one of them spoke a word on the drive back to Myra's. Linda longed for nothing more than to go back to bed.

When they arrived, there seemed to be another party going on. The women were in the kitchen cooking and the men were in the backyard drinking beer, laughing, and telling dirty jokes. Wanting nothing to do with the kitchen, Linda walked out the back door and down the stairs.

Feeling reckless, she helped herself to a beer. Out of the corner of her eye, she saw Donald stiffen, but she didn't care.

Opening the beer, she took a drink, then another, and it wasn't long before the beer chased away the demons that plagued her and she relaxed.

After dinner, Lewis pulled out a camera, saying, "Come on ladies, let's have some fun." Just tipsy enough, Linda let her guard down and joined them, laughing as they posed for several pictures. Gina seemed happy, too, passed from aunt to uncle and everyone in between, until finally, exhausted, she fell asleep.

The evening grew cold and as the beer wore off, the thought of Gina being cold prompted Linda to look for her baby. Finding Gina lying peacefully asleep in Kaitlyn's arms only caused more pain. Grateful Gina was asleep, Linda walked over and said, "Kaitlyn, you're so good with Gina. I hope you and Lewis are plannin' on havin' a family."

Smiling sweetly, Kaitlyn said, "When the time is right, we will. We've only been married a few months, though, so we aren't trying yet."

"If you want my opinion," Linda said. "The trying was the awful part. I didn't mind bein' pregnant, though, and at first I looked forward to having a baby, but I don't seem to be gettin' the hang of motherin'."

"That's silly," Kaitlyn said. "You're doing a fine job."

"Not really," Linda said, "but every single day I pray God will flip a switch and I'll be the momma Gina needs. So far, it ain't happened."

Sweetly, Kaitlyn said, "I don't think you've been a mother long enough to be a good or bad one. I'm sure you just need a little more time. Don't be so hard on yourself. You're doing a great job," Kaitlyn said reassuringly.

Thankful for the kind words, Linda thanked Kaitlyn, saying, "I wish I could believe that," then took her sleeping daughter from Kaitlyn's arms. "I watch you and I see how easy it comes to you. That ain't the case with me. Every day it's a struggle," she said. Then, excusing herself, she walked away.

* * *

The following evening was the wedding reception. Linda brought the only nice dress she owned, the red silky one she bought for the New Year's Eve party. Slipping into the dress, she realized she'd lost more weight than she thought. When she bought the dress, it wasn't snug, now it hung on her. Having brought nothing else to wear, she put on her sweater to hide the dress.

Downstairs, the whole family waited, dressed in their finest. Looking around, she saw Donald holding Gina in his arms. He was smiling at her. Linda smiled back, relaxing a bit.

At the party, they introduced Donald and Linda to Kaitlyn's mom. She was a big lady, with a round face, a smile just as big and a family to rival Myra's.

"It so nice to meet you, Miss Mary," Linda said.

"Hey now," Mary said, "around here everyone just calls me Mom. And who is this little angel you have here?" she asked without taking a breath.

"This is Gina," Linda answered, pulling the blanket back to reveal a sleeping baby.

"What a precious angel," Mary said.

Obviously, Kaitlyn got her mothering instinct from Mary. And again, Linda felt envious of Kaitlyn.

Sitting on the couch, Linda watched as Lewis and Kaitlyn cut their wedding cake, feeding each other sweetly. Kaitlyn was wearing a beautiful off-white silk dress reaching just below her knees. She was tall and thin, her brown hair was long and shiny and it hung in perfect curls that rested gently on her shoulders.

Linda ran her fingers through her own brown hair, thinking of her dull brown eyes, wondering what the hell Donald saw in her. Compared to Kaitlyn, Linda was so plain.

Seeing Donald walk toward her, Linda wished she'd taken more time with herself.

Looking down at her, smiling, Donald said, "You look beautiful tonight." The loving and tender look in his eyes confused her. "Can I get you anything?"

"Is there any beer?" Linda asked.

The Accident

For Donald, the visit home had been restorative and, for a while, things were better between them. Though neither one mentioned it, Linda knew their date night and her heartfelt confession helped, and for a while, she felt stronger. Eventually, though, her strength faded, and the sadness returned.

As the months passed, Linda went from thinking she might have a problem, to knowing she had a problem, to being convinced there was no problem. She was experiencing extreme highs and equally extreme lows. It was impossible to know which way she'd wake up, high or low.

It was on a low day that Donald made the mistake of asking how Linda was.

"I'm tired," Linda answered mechanically. And another fight ensued.

"How can you possibly be tired?" Donald asked. "You sleep all the time."

Instantly defensive, Linda snapped, "I don't sleep all the time."

"You need to get out of the house once in a while," Donald yelled.

Linda shouted back at him, asking. "Why Donald, why do I need to get out of the house if I'm perfectly fine right here?"

When Donald didn't answer, Linda grabbed her cigarettes and walked outside, slamming the screen door, talking out loud to herself, "I'm just fine, damn it. Why the hell won't he leave me alone?"

Sitting down on the stoop, Linda covered her face, crying into her hands.

A few minutes later, she heard the front door open, then close. As the car drove away, Linda lifted her eyes to the heavens, thankful to be alone, saying a quick prayer. She lit a cigarette and walked back into the house and laid down on the couch.

* * *

Gina had started walking just before her birthday was everywhere at once.

"Gina," Linda said, patting the sofa next to her. "Why don't you come on over here and sit with Momma?" Laughing, Gina ran toward the kitchen. Obviously not in a playful mood, it took all she had to get up and chase her daughter.

Trapping Gina between the refrigerator and the back door, Linda scooped her up in her arms, holding her tightly, when she realized she was burning up with fever.

Gina wiggled and cried as Linda took her temperature. Confirming a fever, she gave Gina two baby aspirins. Sitting down on the big girl bed Donald bought for Gina on her birthday, Linda leaned up against the wall rocking Gina, singing whatever pretty song popped into her head until she finally fell asleep.

Feeling sleepy herself but needing to stay close, Linda put Gina in her crib and crawled into her big girl's bed and fell asleep.

It seemed like she'd just closed her eyes when she woke up to Donald standing over her, holding Gina's limp body, screaming, "Linda, wake up! For God's sake, call 911. Something's wrong with Gina."

Realizing she wasn't dreaming, Linda ran to the kitchen and dialed 911. The ambulance arrived within minutes, determining Gina was breathing, though barely. Linda watched in shock as the paramedic put a mask over Gina's tiny mouth. On the other side of the room, Donald talked to another paramedic, explaining that when he got home, he found his wife was asleep and the baby was asleep next to her.

"Wait. That can't be. I put her in her crib," Linda said. "She was running a fever, so I gave her two baby aspirins, then I rocked her to sleep, but I put her down in her crib before I laid down."

"Can I see the bottle of aspirin?" the paramedic asked.

Running into Gina's room, Linda searched frantically for the bottle. She found it under Gina's crib, empty.

With lights and sirens blaring, she sat numb in the front seat, listening to the ambulance driver radio ahead to the hospital, saying they were bringing in a one-year-old overdose. Gina hadn't regained consciousness, and Linda's world was crashing down around her.

When they arrived at the hospital, they whisked Gina away to the emergency room. Crying, Linda said, "Oh my God, this is all my fault. What if I've killed my baby?"

Shaking her roughly by the arms, Donald yelled, with tears in his eyes, "Gina isn't going to die! Don't even say something like that."

While they waited, Linda closed her eyes, bowed her head, and prayed. Praying like she never had before, Linda talked to God, silently pleading with him. "Please God, please allow my baby to be okay. It ain't her fault. It's mine, it's me. I'm a terrible momma. She's a good girl. I know I ain't worthy of your favor, but I'm askin' for it, anyway." She was sitting, rocking back and forth, praying silently, over and over, "Please let my baby be okay," when the doctor walked into the room.

Looking very serious, he said, "The results of your daughter's blood work are back and although we will never know exactly how much aspirin she consumed," he said, "we know it was enough to cause unconsciousness." Shaking his head, he added, "Which is never a good thing."

"Fortunately, Mr. Holloway, you found your daughter before anything worse happened. So far, her blood work looks fine," he said. "We've checked her kidneys and liver for any notable damage, and we see none. I'm sure she is going to be fine, however, I'd like to keep her here overnight for observation."

Linda broke down crying, begging the doctor to let them take Gina home, promising they'd return at once if they noticed any changes in her. Reluctantly, the doctor agreed.

A few minutes later, Donald and Linda walked into the emergency room. Gina was bright eyed, sitting up in the crib clutching her silk blanket and sucking her thumb. She immediately lifted her arms, saying, "Momma." Linda ran over and scooped her up in her arms, hugging her tightly, rocking back and forth, crying softly.

In the car, Linda broke down once again, sobbing uncontrollably.

"Listen, it's over now. Let's just go home," Donald said. "Please, no more tears."

At home, Linda carried Gina into her room, laid her down in her big girl bed and crawled in next to her. The emotions of the day had taken their toll on both Linda and Gina. It didn't take long before they were asleep.

At midnight, Donald came in saying he'd sit with Gina for a while. Linda refused his help and when she woke up again, Gina was nowhere in sight.

Stumbling into the kitchen, she found Gina sitting in her highchair watching cartoons while Donald made breakfast. She poured herself a cup of coffee and sat down at the table.

With her head hung down, Linda sat replaying the day before in her mind. Replaying it detail by detail, she didn't hear Donald calling her.

"Damn it, Linda," Donald shouted. "Answer me."

"I'm sorry. I didn't hear you. What?" she asked.

Donald stared at her intently, but said nothing. Instead, he shook his head, as if disgusted with her, and walked away. No slap in the face could've hurt more, and Linda hung her head, crying once again.

* * *

With a steady stream of tears she hadn't been able to turn off for months now, Linda listened, saying nothing as Donald talked.

His hands felt as cold ice around Linda's wrists as he yanked her up out of her chair yelling at her, "Linda, for God's sake, please stop crying."

The phone forced Donald to let her go. She wondered who he was talking to, but asking required too much effort. Instead, Linda lit a cigarette, walked out the back door, and sat down on the stoop as the details of Gina's accident played over and over in her mind like a terrifying movie, for the thousandth time.

Joining her on the steps, Donald said, "Linda, I'm taking you to see a doctor today. I know you don't want to, but I'm sorry, I can't take this anymore. You need help," he said.

Linda heard him but said nothing. What was there to say? He was right.

An hour later, they were in the car, headed for the doctor's office.

Linda stared out the window with Gina sitting on her lap.

Inside the doctor's office, Linda sat alone, dry-eyed, her head hung down.

"Hello Linda, my name is Dr. Hall. Will you please look at me?" the doctor asked. When Linda didn't answer, he continuing, "Your husband has reached out to me about your state of wellbeing. Can we talk about that?" he asked. Again, Linda said nothing.

"Linda, I know you can hear me," Dr Hall said.

Of course, she could hear him. She could hear all of them. The last few months, Linda had heard nothing else but people talking to her or, better yet, at her.

Donald begging her to talk to him. Her momma telling her to snap out of it, like it was something she had control over. Yes, she heard every question. As far as Linda was concerned, talking wasn't going to change anything. So why the hell should she waste her breath?

Eventually, Dr. Hall gave up and called Donald into the office. "Mr. Holloway, I'm sorry, but I believe your wife is beyond what therapeutic help we can give her. I think a rest is in order."

Donald laughed, saying, "A rest. I don't understand; she sleeps all the time. Isn't there a pill or something you can give her?"

"Linda, will you please look at me?" the doctor asked again. This time Linda raised her head.

Looking her in the eyes, the doctor said, "Linda, I believe you need a break. I would like to send you to a place where you can get some rest. It's a nice place. A place where, when you're ready, there will be people who can help you. Of course, he warned, you'd be away from your daughter and your husband for a time. Then when you get to feeling better, they could come and visit you. What do you think?" he asked.

Linda did not know how she felt about any of it and the silence in the room was making her feel uncomfortable, and once again tears started rolled down her cheeks.

"It's okay, dear. There's no need to answer right now," Dr. Hall said. He turned to Donald and said, "I don't think we should wait on this, Mr. Holloway. I need to make a few calls. I'll be in touch soon."

Linda watched Donald shake the doctor's hand, noticing for the first time he looked tired, too.

Early the next morning, Linda woke to the phone ringing. She stayed awake just long enough to hear Donald say, "Thank you Doctor, I'll get her there," then she drifted back to sleep.

The Sadness and the Sanitarium

In her present state, Linda didn't have a grasp of time as it pertained to her. It could've been days or even weeks before they left for her "rest," as Donald called it.

As Linda sat silently in the front seat, clutching her purse, Donald tried to explain where they were going, but it didn't matter. All Linda knew was she was tired physically and the idea of a "rest" sounded wonderful.

They'd been driving for quite a while when the ocean came into view. Concentrating on the waves washing up onto the shore and then away again, Linda remembered the first time she'd seen the ocean. She could feel the warmth of the water against her skin. She was smiling, lost in thought, when she heard Donald announce their arrival.

They walked in together, holding hands. Linda watched as Donald signed several papers. When he was done, he dropped the pen like it was hot. Then he turned, kissed her on the cheek, and walked away.

With every step Donald took, Linda felt freer. It was like she could breathe for the first time in a long time. She closed her eyes, expecting tears, but none came.

Soon, a nurse came for her. They walked in silence down several halls until they finally stopped in front of a solid gray door.

Inside the room, the air was icy. Shivering, Linda pulled her sweater tighter around herself.

Noticing, the nurse smiled, saying, "You'll get used to it."

Looking around the room, she saw a bed and a nightstand. On the nightstand was a lamp, a clock, and a box of tissues. Across the room was a door to what appeared to be a bathroom. Next to it was a dresser, and a gray metal chair. The tile floor was the same gray as the furniture, with speckles of white throughout.

It was the coldest place she'd ever been, but it matched how she felt inside, cold and gray. The cold made her think again about the warm ocean waters and suddenly she longed for a hot bath.

The nurse's voice brought Linda back from her thoughts. "My name is Melissa. I'm your day nurse." Pointing to a hospital gown and robe folded up on the dresser, the nurse said, "When you're finished unpacking, you can put those on, and I'll be back in a moment."

When Melissa returned, seeing Linda had barely moved since she left, she said, "Here, why don't I help you unpack?" She unpacked Linda's suitcase and put away what little she brought. Next, she helped her undress.

While Linda put on the gown and robe, Melissa filled a glass of water and put it on her nightside. Then she handed her a little white pill, saying, "Take this. It'll help you sleep."

Just as she crawled into the bed, a tall male orderly came in and set a tray of food at the foot of her bed, smiling he said, "Hello, Linda, my name is Vic."

"Okay, you get some rest now," Melissa said as both she and the orderly walked out of the room, closing the door behind them.

Alone in the room, Linda picked at the food and watched as the light outside her window change from cold misty gray to black. The little white pill was making her drowsy, and it wasn't long before she was sound asleep.

* * *

On her third day at the sanitarium, Linda got up and showered. She dressed in a pair of blue slacks, a white button-down blouse, and black leather loafers, then she set off to familiarize herself with her new home.

Outside, she sat on a nearby bench, with her back to the sanitarium. It sat high above the ocean and the views were more beautiful than anything she'd ever seen. She couldn't help wondering if this was what Heaven looked like. Closing her eyes, she could hear the wind as it moved through the trees and felt the cool breeze as it touched her gently on the face.

Opening her eyes and looking to her left, she saw a vast forest of redwood trees stretching for what seemed like miles. It reminded her of a lush green carpet, and she longed to run barefoot through it in wild abandon. To her right, she saw an equally beautiful valley. Throughout the valley, there were rows and rows of trees. Their leaves were changing with the coming fall from green to beautiful yellows, oranges, and reds. And beyond the trees appeared to be tiny mansions all in a row.

Looking straight ahead, Linda could see the ocean and watched as the water smashed up against craggy cliffs. Below the cliffs was a golden sandy beach and above it, the softest, fluffiest white clouds.

Maybe, just maybe, if I look really close, I'll see angels sitting upon the clouds, playin' their harps, Linda thought, convinced this was Heaven.

Inside, there was a large sitting room with floor to ceiling windows. Across the room, she saw doors leading to another garden. Scattered around were high-backed leather chairs and couches, some occupied with other patients.

Four hallways jetted off from the sitting room: two to the left of the windows and two to the right. She set out to explore them. To her delight, at the end of hallway number four, she was greeted with aromas of the dining room.

Mimicking those in the room, Linda picked up a tray and walked through the line. Though the food smelled delicious, she did not know what most of it was, so she chose a ham sandwich on white bread, a bag of potato chip and a Coke. Then, taking her tray, she sat down at a table alone.

She could see the beach in the distance and thought of her parents. She wondered if her momma and daddy knew where she was.

And if they did, what did they think? Were they disappointed in her? She was sure they must be because she was disappointed her in herself.

Dear God, what in the world's wrong with me? Linda thought, as the questions flooded in like the waves on the beach, one after the other.

Why did she feel better without Donald and Gina? And why wasn't she happy? Where did she lose herself? Had she ever known herself? So many questions, and right now she had no answers, but hoped this was where she was going to find them.

* * *

When she arrived back in her room, a man was sitting in the chair next to the dresser. He wore a long white coat and held a metal clipboard.

Standing up with his hand outstretched, he said, "Hello, my name is Dr. Bob. Do I have the pleasure of meeting Mrs. Holloway?"

Linda nodded and shook his hand.

"May I call you Linda?" Dr. Bob asked. Then, without waiting for her answer, he said, "I was hoping we could go for a walk and talk today."

Linda would rather have laid down and slept, but curious about Dr. Bob, she nodded yes.

Together, they walked and as they walked, Dr. Bob talked, and Linda listened.

"I know you've been here for a few days, and I would have come sooner, but I wanted to give you time to rest and get acquainted with the facility. I'm hopeful we can start your treatments tomorrow," he said. "What do you think?"

The word treatment caused Linda to panic. Grabbing ahold of her arm, Dr. Bob looked straight into her eyes and said, "It's okay. I know you're scared, but I think I can help you if you'll let me. Will you let me?" he asked.

As Linda struggled, pulling away, Dr. Bob held on tight, saying, "It's okay, you don't have to answer right now. Let's continue our walk, shall we?" he said, gently letting go of her.

As they walked, hall by hall, once again Dr. Bob talked and Linda quietly listened. In hall one, the doctor explained, "These rooms are where you will eventually attend meetings." Entering hall number two, he said, "In this hall we offer academic classes. You're welcome to attend if you're interested." And in hall number three, their walk ended in front of door number seven. Dr. Bob turned to Linda, saying, "Thank you for walking with me. Shall we meet here again tomorrow at 10am?"

Maintaining her silence, Linda nodded, indicating she'd be there.

"Okay, until then," Dr. Bob said, as he closed the door behind him.

* * *

The following morning, and every morning after, Linda was in Dr. Bob's office at 10:00 am. At first, Dr. Bob talked, and Linda listened.

He never pushed her to talk, but occasionally, he'd stop and ask her a question. When she didn't answer, he simply went on talking as if she wasn't there at all.

He talked mostly about himself, where he lived as a child, about his parents, his siblings and where he attended college. He talked about his family, saying, "Someday, when you're ready, I'd love to hear about your family."

Every morning, after eating, she would shower before going to see Dr. Bob. In Linda's opinion, showering every day when you did nothing at all was just plain stupid. However, the nurses insisted, so she did it. The food at the facility was boring, so Linda ate very little and the hour she spent with Dr. Bob was an exercise in torture.

On the inside, Linda wanted to talk. She tried, really tried, but just couldn't. So, day after day, Dr. Bob talked and Linda listened. Until the day Dr. Bob said, "I got a phone call today from your husband asking if he could come and visit you."

Her head snapped up and before she could control herself, she asked, "What did you tell him?" hoping he'd said no.

Smiling, Dr. Bob answered, "I told him it was up to you."

"I ain't ready, Dr. Bob," Linda said.

"Why don't you want to see your husband?" he asked.

Unable to put her reasons into words, she just said, "I just don't wanna."

"Okay Linda, I won't press you now. You think about it, and we can talk more tomorrow," he said, smiling.

Realizing those were the first words she'd spoken since coming to the sanitarium, Linda nodded, silent again, wondering if he'd tricked her.

Maybe Dr. Bob had lied about Donald asking to see her, but Linda hadn't lied. She wasn't ready to see Donald, not yet.

* * *

From her first night in the facility and each night since, the little white pill came, and every night Linda refused it. And every night the nurse insisted, saying, "It's doctor's orders." The pills were so strong they made it impossible for her to move her head no matter how hard she tried and her eyes crossed, making it impossible to focus.

Then sleep would come, followed by dreams. Each night's dream started out differently, but they all ended the same, with Donald standing at the foot of her bed, holding Gina's lifeless body.

She'd just awakened from yet another dream and lay with tears rolling down her face when she heard the door to her room open and close. When a low light flooded the room, her eyes flew open in shock.

Standing above her was a tall man. Although Linda hadn't seen him since the day they'd admitted her into the sanitarium, she recognized Vic immediately.

She tried to lift her head but couldn't. She struggled, trying to sit up and couldn't because her arms were restrained. Looking down, she saw her legs spread wide apart, tied to the rails. Realizing Vic's intent, Linda opened her mouth to scream, but his hand quickly covered it. He looked her straight in the eyes and shook his head from side to side, telling her without words she better not try to scream again.

His saliva was hot and sticky, and he smelled of sweat and stale cigarettes. Her stomach rolled as the taste of vomit rose to her throat. Gripped with fear, knowing she was helpless, she closed her eyes tight, trying not to focus on what was happening to her. Instead, Linda allowed herself to travel back in her mind…soon she was back with her family in the station wagon, singing as loud as she could, trying to outdo them all.

What's the name of that song? Oh, I know I know it, she thought, trying to escape the feel of his mouth on her breast, as the tears rolled down her face. He tried to kiss her on the mouth. Recoiling, Linda turned her face. As if punishing her for resisting his kiss, he tortured her further, moving his hands slowly down her now naked body.

In a rage, she opened her eyes and saw Vic looking down at her laughing. Linda wanted to scream, scratch his eyes out, kick him, but tied down and drugged, there was nothing she could do. She watched in horror as he climbed up on the bed between her legs.

Paralyzed with fear, she squeezed her eyes shut, rocking her head back and forth, crying, wishing she could will herself to die. She felt his release and heard him zip his pants as she prayed for God to take her from this miserable existence.

He grabbed a hold of her face, squeezing her jaw tight. Using his fingers, he forced her mouth open and shoved in another white pill. Squeezing her jaw even tighter, he whispered, "You will tell no one."

He untied her feet and wrists and drew the sheet up over her. She heard the click of the door as he closed it softly behind him.

In the pitch black, shivering, Linda held the pill between her teeth and thought about spitting it out, but instead she swallowed it, praying it would take hold of her quickly. Rolling over onto her side, she drew her legs up to her chin, clutched her stomach, and rocked back and forth, praying,

Over and over she prayed, "Please God, please take me away from this miserable existence." She cried, begging God to release her from her earthly body until finally the pill took effect and once again, she slept.

With Linda's list of terrifying dreams now expanded, she saw him, smelled him, and could even taste his vileness as he raped her again, laughing. She woke up terrified. Rolling to her side, she relieved her gagging onto the floor below her, then slept again.

* * *

When Linda appeared in Dr. Bob's office the next morning, she shouted, abruptly, "I wanna go home. NOW!"

Dr Bob pointed to the chair across from him, saying, "That's impossible. Now sit down."

"Impossible?" she asked. "Why is it impossible for me to go home?"

"Because your husband committed you," Dr. Bob answered. "And I am sorry, but you can't go anywhere until he rescinds your commitment." He pointed again to the chair and said, "Please sit down."

Instead of sitting down, Linda turned and walked out.

For the next few weeks, Linda continued to plead with Dr. Bob to let her go home. Desperate, she even thought about telling Dr. Bob about Vic's nightly visits.

"Can't you just tell Donald I'm better?" Linda begged Dr. Bob.

"No dear, I am sorry I can't do that," he said, explaining she hadn't even started her meetings yet.

"I have another medication I want you to try," he said.

"NO, please. No more pills. I don't like the way they make me feel. Please, Dr. Bob, please send me home," Linda pleaded.

"Linda, if you intend to get out of here, then you must take the medications and put in the time. However, if you continue to refuse the medications and won't go to the meetings, then going home may not be possible."

"Are you saying I may never get out of here?" Linda asked.

"Yes, that's exactly what I am saying," Dr. Bob answered.

Linda sat quietly, weighing her options. Then said, "Okay, if it's the only way out of here, then I guess it's what I gotta do."

Smiling, Dr. Bob asked, "Then don't you have a meeting to attend?"

Shock Therapy

As Dr. Bob suggested, Linda went to the meetings, took her day pills, and spent more time outside. And she made a new friend. her name was Beth.

Beth appeared to be Linda's age, but very childlike. She babbled on about senseless things. When Linda asked her simple things, like her name, or her favorite color, or what she had for breakfast, Beth answered, never looking directly at Linda.

They were an odd pair, but they worked. Neither one really cared about what the other one said. Beth talked about her imaginary friends, her stuffed rabbit Rocco, and about what she was having for dinner. Linda talked about anything and everything. She told Beth about Donald and Gina, and how she hoped one day to go home to them. She told her about her momma and daddy, and how much she missed them. Sitting on a bench, Beth rock backed and forth to the sound of Linda's voice. Thinking she might like some music to rock to, and happy for the first time in a long time, Linda sang.

* * *

Linda had given up ever leaving the sanitarium when Dr. Bob said, "Linda, I have a treatment that I think will help you. It's called Electroconvulsive Therapy," he said. "For short, let's call it shock therapy. It's administered by a series of electrical shocks that will penetrate your skull, going into your brain through probes attached to certain areas of your head."

Sitting up on the edge of her seat, Linda cut Dr. Bob off, asking, "Why in the hell would I let you do somethin' like that?"

Not responding to her question, Dr Bob repeated himself saying, "It's administered by a series of electrical shocks that penetrate your skull, going into your brain through probes attached to certain areas of your head and if successful, it could reverse your mental condition," he said.

This being the first time she'd heard the words "mental condition" mentioned, Linda asked, "What mental condition are you talkin' about?"

Did he really think she was crazy? she thought. *Maybe I am crazy. I allowed myself to be married to a boy I didn't know or even like.* Which sounded crazy to her.

The fact she'd let her momma convince her to have a baby when she knew she didn't want one sounded crazy, too. And certainly, only someone with a mental condition would almost kill their own baby. Right? And if it was true, and she was crazy, then maybe for everyone's sake she should stay in the sanitarium. *After all,* she thought, *it wasn't so bad. At least there was no cleaning or laundry to do.*

Then Vic's face flashed before her eyes and the thought of his nightly abuse caused chills to race down her spine. No, staying here was definitely not an option.

The idea of probes attached to her head with electrical shocks shooting into her brain terrified her, but the possibility of never getting out of the sanitarium terrified her more. "Okay, if you think it'll help. I'll do it," Linda said.

* * *

The day of her first treatment, after giving her a sedative, they wheeled down hall number three to a cold sterile room, and placed her on a cold metal bed. She felt a hot burning sensation run up her arm. Then nothing.

She woke up hours later, alone in her room, with a headache and an overwhelming feeling of despair.

Her treatments were every other day for two weeks. On non-treatment days, she went to meetings. The group meetings weren't bad, mostly, Linda listened with half an ear. So far, she hadn't been called on to speak. Until today.

"How about you, Linda?" Brenda asked. "Would you like to share today?"

All heads turned in her direction and all eyes focused on her. She reeled from that one nonspecific question; would she like to share? Share what? Feeling sick to her stomach, panicking, Linda looked toward the door and thought about leaving.

"Maybe I should be more specific. Linda, do you know what brought you here to the sanitarium?" the therapist asked.

Sitting with her head down, Linda whispered angrily, "Of course I do."

"Can you tell us why?" Brenda asked.

Again, Linda looked toward the door, but she knew better than anyone there was nowhere to go. Deep down inside, she also knew if she was ever going to get out of this place, she needed to talk about it, so she answered, "It's because I almost killed my baby," bursting into tears.

Brenda excused the group and sat down in the chair next to her, holding Linda's hand as she cried. "Linda, you're going to be okay," she said.

* * *

As the weeks passed, her treatments continued, and Linda made progress. Brenda explained how the guilt of Gina's accident had taken hold and consumed her.

"In part," Brenda said, "your mother was right, Linda. Some women experience a type of depression, and usually, it passes quickly. However, on occasions, when the hormones in your body don't return to a proper balance after giving birth, what is called postpartum depression sets in. Left untreated, it can lead to a serious mental breakdown.

"In your case, the good news is that you have nothing to feel guilty about. Your daughter didn't die. She's alive, and she wants her momma to come home. I know it won't be easy, Linda, but if you think you're ready, I know I can help you. It will require work on your part, though."

The idea of being home and of being alone with Gina made Linda wonder if she'd ever be ready. She sat, head down, not speaking, listening intently to every word Brenda said.

"You'll have to do this on your own, Linda," Brenda said. "This isn't something anyone can do for you, and it will be hard."

Looking up, with tears in her eyes, Linda asked, "What do I got to do?"

"You'd have to forgive yourself," Brenda said.

"Is that all I gotta do?" she asked.

"No, there's more," Brenda said. "You also have to forgive your husband and your mother for the parts you feel they played in your being here and you must take full responsibility," she answered.

"I can forgive my momma and Donald. That's easy, 'cause it wasn't their fault. It was my fault," Linda said.

"Oh, the thought of forgiving others may seem easy," Brenda said, "but it's not. Because before you can forgive anyone else, you must forgive yourself first."

"How do I do that?" Linda asked.

"Forgiving yourself requires being honest, admitting your shortcomings, accepting you, and loving you," Brenda said.

Linda's heart was breaking as the memories flashed before her eyes. Donald holding Gina's listless body, the sight of the oxygen mask covering her tiny face. The paramedics, the ambulance ride and the penetrating silence after the radio went silent. Knowing Gina could've died and the guilt that came with it was something Linda knew she'd have to fight and fight hard if she was going to survive.

Sobbing now, she asked, "How can I ever forgive myself for nearly killing my baby? Please tell me how?" she begged.

"Did you intentionally leave the aspirin bottle out for Gina to find?" Brenda asked.

Tearing up, Linda answered, "Of course not."

"And you didn't intend to hurt your baby, did you?" she asked.

"No, I never meant to hurt Gina," Linda said, "but I am scared. I don't trust myself. What if I hurt her again? The thought of hurting her again scares me to death," she admitted.

"I know you blame yourself, but accidents happen all the time, even the very best of parents, and I think you've learned from what happened and you'd never allow it to happen again. Am I right?" Brenda asked.

"You make it sound so easy," Linda said, blowing her nose.

"No, Linda," Brenda said, "I already guaranteed you this would not be easy, remember? However, it is essential for your emotional healing."

* * *

Leaving therapy, grateful and with newfound determination, Linda wrapped her arms around her body, hugging herself tight. She felt warm inside, almost giddy with happiness. She felt like she could finally see light at the end of her very long and dark tunnel.

Back in her room, knowing that forgiving herself was going to be the hardest thing she'd ever done, Linda knelt down on the hard, cold grey floor next to her bed and prayed like she'd never prayed before.

"Dear God, I wanna go home. Deep in my heart, I really do, but I'm terrified. How can I trust myself with Gina? She is so little and so fragile. I know I didn't intend to hurt her, but I did and before I could ever forgive myself; I need to ask for your forgiveness. Please forgive me for not being a good momma. I know I shouldn't have had a baby, but I did, and I can't go back now. So, I need your help. Give me the strength to get better so I can go home to my baby. Amen."

* * *

Determined to fight Vic if he came to her room, Linda pretended to take her nighttime pill. Then, after the nurse left, she flushed it down the toilet. The windows of the facility were barred, for obvious reasons, but a small handle turned to let in air. Unable to sleep, Linda sat in front of the open window.

Taking a deep breath, she inhaled the cold air, allowing it to fill her lungs, releasing it as she allowed the emotions of the day to return.

While she was happy the faceless demon who'd tormented her for almost three years finally had a name, and she wasn't crazy, Linda felt sad, too. Sad she hadn't been a better wife to Donald and that she'd missed so much time with Gina. Refusing to focus on the sadness, Linda looked forward to her ten o'clock appointment with Dr. Bob the next morning. She couldn't wait to share with him her newfound happiness and her hope for the future. With a goal set to do exactly as Brenda suggested, Linda couldn't wait to get out of here. She longed to go home and make up for lost time.

She was smiling, thinking happy thoughts, and feeling the ocean air as it caressed her face when she heard the familiar opening of the door to her room, then the soft closing. She could see the look on Vic's face when he realized she wasn't in her bed. She watched as he looked frantically around for her.

Linda froze as his eyes found hers.

Storming across the room, he grabbed her by the hair and dragged her across the room, flinging her up on the bed like a rag doll.

In the process, her foot contacted Vic's groin. She watched as, first in shock, then in pain, Vic doubled over and fell to the floor. Jumping off the bed, Linda ran to the door. Not stopping to see if anyone was in the hall and certainly not caring either, she ran as quickly and as quietly as she could to the common room. The room was dark and empty, and she ran to a large chair and dove in.

There she waited, barely breathing, praying Vic wouldn't discover her hiding place and drag her back to her room, where he'd rape her more violently than ever.

Linda smelled him before she saw him. The smell of his unwashed body, stale cigarettes and sick sexual arousal were smells she was sure she'd never forget. Burying her face deeper into the chair, she prayed harder. To her surprise, just as she was sure he was about to find her, Vic turned and walked away from her.

Linda waited for a long time to be sure he wasn't coming back before she tiptoed back to her room.

There, she slipped quietly between the sheets and pulled the blanket over her head, praying with all her might God would answer her prayers and she could go home soon.

With each passing week, Linda got stronger. And when Dr. Bob hinted at the possibly of her going home soon, she cried, this time tears of joy as she prayed, thanking God for answering her prayers.

Vic hadn't returned to her room.

* * *

Then the day came that Linda both hoped for and dreaded.

"Linda, you need to know I've made arranged for Donald to come and visit you," Dr. Bob said.

"Do you think he will bring Gina with him?" Linda asked.

"I believe he said he was. Unless you don't want to see her?" Doctor Bob asked. "I can ask him not to."

"No, please don't, Dr. Bob," she said. "Please, I need to see her."

When the day arrived, Linda put on her white button-down blouse, black slacks, and black leather slip-on shoes.

Without benefit of a mirror, she combed her hair, tucking it back behind her ears. Then she picked up her sweater and headed down to the common area to wait for Donald and Gina to arrive. Pacing back and forth, more nervous than she ever remembered being, Linda had begun to wonder if Donald was even coming when she heard her name called.

"Linda, you have visitors," the nurse said. "Would you like to visit them here, or in the garden?" she asked.

"It's a beautiful day today. I think Gina would love the gardens," Linda answered.

"Okay, you wait here while l take them to the gardens. Then I'll return for you," she said.

* * *

Standing in front of the window, she took a long look at herself. The reflection she saw didn't seem familiar to her. Her eyes seemed lifeless, her color pale. She looked like she'd been ill, and even though she'd gained some weight, her clothes hung on her. How long had she been here? She wasn't sure, but it seemed like years.

The sound of the nurse's voice saying, "Linda, your family is waiting. Are you ready?" drew her attention back to the present.

Linda followed the nurse down hall number one and through the library. Stopping at a small gray door in the very back of the room, using a key, the nurse unlocked the door and pushed it open, revealing a beautiful garden.

"This is a private garden. We only use it when the families come to visit the patients. Isn't it beautiful?" the nurse asked.

The garden was pretty, but being on the east side of the building, even though the sun was shining, it was cold. She had the feeling they did not use this garden much.

She saw Donald sitting alone. Initially panicking, she looked around for Gina, thinking maybe he hadn't brought her after all.

Then she saw her daughter running toward her. She was wearing a pink dress and her hair was long now. Running as fast as her legs would take her, Gina screamed, "Momma!"

Linda bend down as Gina ran into her in her arms and held her tight. Pulling back from Gina's embrace, with tears in her eyes, she inspected her daughter.

Her hair was now a beautiful strawberry blond and her eyes had finally settled on a color. Hazel, just like Linda's. With that exception, in every other way, Gina resembled her father.

"Look at you. I think you've grown a foot. How old are you now?" Linda asked.

"I am almost this many," Gina said, holding up three tiny fingers.

Unable to do the math in her head, her best guess was she'd been there for sixteen months.

Trying not to cry, Linda asked, "Have you been a good girl for your daddy?" Gina nodded yes and hugged Linda again, this time tighter.

Looking up, Linda found Donald staring at her intently, causing her to blush a bit as he walked over and put his arms around her.

"I've missed you. How've you been?" he asked.

Linda felt the anger boil up inside her. Her first instinct was to ask him how the hell he thought she'd been? After all, she'd been here for what felt like years. She'd been drugged, raped, and was now enduring treatments which left her physically sick for days. Linda ignored his question and asked one of her own.

"When do I get to leave here?" Linda asked.

"That's up to you, Linda," Donald answered. "Well, it's up to you and your doctor. You can come home whenever he says you're ready."

Really, Donald, is that true? Is it really up to me? Is what Linda wanted to ask. Not ready for him to know she knew he'd signed her commitment papers, she asked, "How've you been?"

Donald seemed changed, withdrawn and suddenly a thought, too frightening to even consider, flashed through Linda's mind. What if he didn't want her to come home? What if he couldn't trust her with Gina and he left her here forever?

With sad cow eyes, Donald answered, "I'm okay." Taking her by the arm, he led her to a table in the sun. Looking back to make sure Gina was following them, she smiled, watching Gina skip and hop along behind them. She couldn't help but envy Gina's obvious joy with life.

They sat in the garden talking and playing with Gina until lunchtime. When she had finished eating, Gina climbed up into Linda's lap.

"Is she too heavy?" Donald asked. "I can take her."

Laughing, Linda said, "Yes, but please don't take her yet."

Within minutes, Gina fell asleep and reluctantly, Linda laid her down on a nearby couch, then sat down beside her. Taking Linda's hand, Donald kissed it sweetly. Not trusting her feelings, she pulled her hand away. It had been a wonderful day, and she didn't want to be confused by Donald's sad eyes and sweet words.

"We better get going now," Donald said. "It's a long drive home."

Linda was sobbing openly as she watched Donald walk away carrying their still sleeping daughter in his arms. It took everything she had not to run after him and beg him to take her with them.

Though she knew she wasn't ready to go home yet, she was sure that once she did, she wouldn't ever be coming back. *I'd rather die than spend one minute more than is necessary in this godforsaken place*, she thought to herself as she blew her nose.

Rising, her legs trembled as tears rolled down her cheeks. Her arms felt empty and her heart was breaking. Whispering out loud, Linda said, "I promise you, baby girl, momma is gonna work even harder so I can come home to you soon."

* * *

And then that day came.

"Linda," Dr. Bob said, "I think it's time we talk about your going home."

"Do you really think I'm ready, Dr. Bob?" Linda asked.

"I think the better question is, do you think you're ready?" Dr. Bob asked.

Searching deep down in her heart and soul, she knew the answer was yes! Yes, because now she could see that her being here had nothing to do with the fact she couldn't cope. It was because her body wasn't functioning properly. She'd taken full responsibility for Gina's accident. And she knew now that if she'd gotten the help she needed, despite what her momma or Donald said, none of this would've happened.

Without hesitation, Linda said, "Yes, Dr. Bob I do."

"And so do I," he said, adding, "I think you have a phone call to make."

With her heart beating frantically, she dialed her own telephone number. She let it ring three times and was about to hang-up when she heard Donald's voice say, "Hello."

Suddenly, her throat went dry, and she lost her voice.

"Hello," Donald said again louder, asking, "is anyone there?"

Finally, she whispered, "Hello Donald. It's me, Linda."

"Who is this? Speak up? I can't hear you," Donald yelled into the phone.

"It's me," Linda said louder. Then she blurted out, "I wanna come home now."

Linda could hear Donald breathing, but he said nothing.

"Did you hear me, Donald?" Linda asked.

"Yes, I heard you. Are you sure?" Donald asked.

"Yes Donald, I am sure," Linda answered. "I've gone to my meetings and I'm taking my medications. My treatments are done and Dr. Bob says I'm ready to go home."

"Then I'll call Dr. Bob and check with him," Donald said. "If he agrees you're ready, I'll make plans to come get you."

Feeling relieved Donald hadn't fought her on coming home and feeling braver, Linda asked, "Is Gina there? Can I talk to her?"

"Gina, honey, your momma is on the phone. Hurry," Donald said.

"Hi, Momma," Gina said so sweetly Linda thought she might die on the spot.

"Hi, Gina. How are you, sweetheart?" Linda asked, with tears welling up in her eyes.

"Fine, I'm playing with the new doll Susie bought for me." Gina said.

Linda was about to ask who Susie was when Donald came back on the line.

"Okay," Donald said, "I'll call the doctor and see what he says," obviously about to hang up.

"Wait Donald, who's Susie?" Linda asked.

Donald laughed nervously, repeating her question, "Who's Susie?"

"Yes Donald. Who is Susie?" she asked again.

"Susie is the lady I pay to take care of Gina during the day while I work," he said, sounding defensive.

"And does she take care of you at night, Donald?" Linda asked.

"I have to work, Linda, so I hired someone to take care of Gina," Donald answered.

"Or did you hire someone to replace me?" Linda asked.

Sounding sincere, Donald said, "Linda, no one can replace you."

Taking a deep breath and exhaling, Linda said, "I know I haven't been a good wife and I wouldn't blame you if you replaced me."

"Well, I haven't. Now say goodbye so I can call Dr. Bob." Donald said.

"Okay, goodbye Donald," Linda said, hanging up. Smiling, she walked back to her room, feeling hopeful for the first time in ages.

Going Home

Poised on the edge of one of the overstuffed chairs in the lobby, Linda waited for Donald to come to take her home. She was nervous, but looking forward to seeing Gina, but when Donald arrived, she wasn't with him.

Looking around, she asked, "Where's Gina? Didn't you bring her with you?"

"No, I thought you and I would take our time getting back home. Gina's staying with friends for a few days," Donald answered.

"Oh, is she with Susie?" Linda asked.

"No, Susie only works during the week," Donald answered right away. "I left Gina with the wife of a friend. Does that make you feel better?"

"No, I'd feel better if she were here with us," Linda said.

"I know," Donald said, "come on, let's get you out of here."

When they arrived at Dr. Bob's office, all the papers were ready to sign, and just before signing them, Donald looked up at her and asked, "Are you sure, Linda?"

Sounding more confident than she felt, Linda said, "Yes, I'm ready to go home."

To her delight as they drove away, Donald turned on the radio to a country station. Just like old times, Linda reached into the glove box and pulled out a cigarette. Lighting two, she handed one to Donald, asking sweetly, "Donald, can we just go home now? No surprises?"

Donald agreed, no surprises, but insisted they stop at a hotel for the night when it got dark.

They stopped on a dark road in a dumpy town somewhere between the sanitarium and home. Linda was tired and wanted to go right to sleep. That way, when she woke up, they'd be on their way home. And she would be on her way back to Gina. Hungry, Donald suggested they eat dinner first.

They found a small Mexican restaurant where Donald ordered the tamale plate special and two beers.

"Donald, please," Linda said. "We don't need beer."

"Why not? After all, we're celebrating," Donald said.

"Seriously, Donald," Linda whispered across the table. "I hardly think my gettin' out of the nuthouse is anything worth celebratin'."

"We're not celebrating you getting out of the nuthouse, silly. We're celebrating your birthday," Donald said.

Painfully aware she didn't know what the date was, Linda asked, "Is today my birthday?"

"No, not today," Donald said. "It was a few weeks ago, your 22nd."

There's another thing I missed, she thought sadly to herself. "Then I guess we should celebrate," she said.

Linda wasted no time finishing her beer, then reached for Donald's, reminding him after all it was her birthday celebration.

Walking to the car, she stumbled. Laughing, she said, "I think I am a bit tipsy."

Opening the car door for her, laughing, Donald said, "I see that."

In their hotel room, in the sweetest voice she'd ever heard, Donald asked, "Can I make love to you?"

The idea of sex with Donald or anybody sickened her to the core and suddenly Linda wondered if she'd made a mistake leaving the sanitarium.

Grateful for the alcohol running through her veins, Linda allowed Donald to touch her. All the while trying to chase away the memory of Vic and praying, Donald did not notice her stiffen as he placed his mouth, all too familiarly, on her breast.

* * *

Arriving at the home of Donald's friends, Linda asked, "Who are these people?"

"Dave and I work together. His wife, Diane, offered to watch Gina for me." Donald answered.

It mortified Linda, knowing they knew where she'd been. Knew about her illness, and worse, what lead up to it.

Putting his arm around her shoulders, Donald said, "Don't worry, David and Diane are good people. You're going to like them."

As Diane opened the door, all at once, there was chaos. The sound of a dog barking and kids playing in the yard was music to her ears, and she relaxed.

Gina came running in, yelling, "Momma, Momma," and jumped in Linda's arms, seemingly happy to see her, which caused Linda's eyes to fill with tears.

Linda buried her head in her daughter's neck. Gina wiggled, wanting to get down.

Closing her eyes, Linda silently thanked God for his blessings, for taking care of Gina and for seeing her through the past eighteen months of her life.

"Lord," she prayed, "Please help me be the momma Gina needs now and please help me learn to love my husband. Mostly, God, please give me strength to be the best I can be one day at a time."

And God answered her prayers. Linda got stronger and more confident daily. She no longer desired to lay in bed all day. She got up early and spent her days caring for the house and Gina. Content.

* * *

When she went into the sanitarium, Gina was barely a year and a half old. Now she was an articulate, busy three-year-old who'd developed her own little personality.

At two feet tall, she was all girl and loved to play dress up and wear the plastic toy jewels Donald bought her. And she carried the doll Susie gave her everywhere she went. She was everywhere at once and full of questions.

Lying on her belly coloring in her color book while watching Romper Room, Gina asked, "Hey Momma, where did Susie go? I miss her."

"Susie was only here taking care of you while Momma was gone," Linda answered.

Susie had offered to continue working for them, but Linda begged Donald to let her try to take care of the house and Gina by herself, promising if she felt overwhelmed at all, she'd let him know. The thought of Susie taking care of Gina, the house and possibly Donald drove her to do her best.

"Why did Susie take care of me?" Gina asked.

"Because I was sick," Linda explained.

Looking very concerned, Gina turned from the TV and asked, "What was wrong with you, Momma?"

Unsure how to explain her illness to a three-year-old, Linda got up from her chair, walked over and laid down on the floor next to Gina and asked, "Gina baby, would it be okay if we just say Momma was away for a little while, and now, she has come back?"

"Are you still sick?" Gina asked.

"No, I'm not all the way better, but I'm gettin' there," Linda answered.

"Are you going to leave again?" Gina asked.

"Not if I can help it," Linda said, meaning it.

"Okay, can I go outside and play now?" Gina asked, but was out the door before Linda could answer.

At night in their bed, when Donald reached for her, Linda used the same technique she used when Vic visited her room. She'd closed her eyes tight and visualize herself somewhere else. She'd see herself running through a dry riverbed with her siblings on a hot day or in the back seat of her daddy's station wagon, singing.

If Donald knew she wasn't present during their lovemaking, he didn't mention it. And afterwards, she'd fall asleep quickly only to wake up in a cold sweat from another bad dream where she'd lay awake for hours, afraid of the dreams she knew would come again when she closed her eyes.

With an active three-year-old and a house to care for, it wasn't long before once again Linda was exhausted. Worried, she made an appointment with Doctor Hall and reluctantly called Susie, asking if she could come and sit with Gina.

The day of her appointment, Linda answered the front door, pleasantly surprised to find that Susie was nothing like she had envisioned her. She was a sweet older lady, probably in her sixties. She reminded her of her momma. She instantly felt bad for accusing Donald of infidelity.

Looking happy to see her, Dr. Hall asked, "What brings you in today, Mrs. Holloway?"

"I ain't sleeping good," Linda answered. "I'm busy all day and even though I feel tired at night, when I lie down, I can't sleep." Not mentioning the nightly dreams, she said, "I'm worried the depression will return."

"Is there something bothering you?" Dr Hall asked.

Linda hesitated, thinking about Vic. Maybe she should tell someone about her time in the sanitarium, but quickly changed her mind.

Lying, Linda answered, saying, "No, Dr. Hall, everything is fine. I just can't sleep."

"Are you taking the medication they prescribed when you came home?" he asked.

"They didn't give me no medication," Linda answered.

"Well then, that's good," Dr. Hall said in a kind and reassuring voice. "Obviously, your doctor thought you didn't need medication. And being busy all day and chasing a three-year-old can't be easy without sleep. Given enough time, I am sure you'll adjust. However, just in case, I'm going to give you a prescription for a sleep aid. I will leave it up to you if you use it or not, but if it gets bad and you can't sleep, take one at bedtime," he said, adding, "and I think maybe you should consider some ongoing therapy."

Leaving, Linda thanked him, promising to give the therapy some thought.

She stopped at the pharmacy and filled the prescription. At home, she put the bottle of pills in the medicine chest, way up high where Gina couldn't reach them.

* * *

Linda had been home for several months and still had not called her momma nor her sister. She knew she should, but she wasn't ready to hear the pity in their voices.

So, when Donald reminded her to call her mother again for the tenth time, defensively Linda responded, saying, "I've been home for months. Why hasn't she called me?"

"That's my fault. I asked her to wait," Donald explained. "I thought you'd call them when you were ready. I just didn't think it would take you this long."

Pouring a cup of coffee, Linda said, "Okay, I promise I will call her."

When Linda called, her momma answered the phone saying "Hello, who is this?" she was slurring her words.

Looking at the clock and realizing she was obviously drunk at 10 o'clock in the morning, Linda asked, "Momma, have you been drinkin'?"

"Of course not," her momma answered, but Linda knew she was lying.

"Where's daddy?" Linda asked.

"Your daddy's at the bar," her momma said. "That's why I'm drinkin'."

"You just said you weren't drinkin'," Linda reminded her.

Her momma said, "Well, I am, and it's 'cause your daddy's at the bar all the time and if he's gonna drink, then I am, too."

"Why ain't daddy workin'?" Linda asked.

Blowing her nose, Momma said, "He got laid off over a month ago, and he ain't been home since."

"Hey, Momma, I just called to tell ya'll I'm home. Gina just woke up from her nap, so I gotta run. I'll call back later," Linda said, hanging up the phone, thankful they'd never gotten around to talking about her.

Vietnam

Bursting through the screen, nearly ripping it from the hinges, Gina came running into the house, screaming at the top of her lungs, "Momma, can I have an apple?" as she climbed up on a dining room chair to work on her puzzle.

Taking an apple from the fruit bowl, Linda said, "Okay, stay here. I'll go peel it." She was almost to the kitchen when she heard the screen door open again.

Seeing Donald walk through the door in the middle of the day was certainly a concern. What concerned her more was the look on his face.

"Look, Daddy, my puzzle's almost done," Gina announced proudly.

Linda watched Donald as walked to the table. He looked at Gina's puzzle, then patted her on the head, saying, "I need to talk to your momma. You run along and play outside now."

Worrying about Gina being outside without her, Linda said, "No, Gina, you stay right here and work on your puzzle. Your daddy and I'll be outside on the front porch if you need us."

Putting the apple back in the fruit bowl, Linda grabbed her cigarettes and followed Donald out to the porch. As she waited for Donald to speak, Linda lit a cigarette and offered it to him, then lit one for herself and sat down on the stoop.

After several drags off the cigarette, Donald said, "They're finally sending me to Vietnam."

Much calmer than she felt, Linda asked, "When?"

"I don't have an exact day yet," Donald answered. "All I know is they're transferring us to Hawaii first."

"Transferring us to Hawaii? Why?" Linda asked.

"I do not know. I only know when I leave for Vietnam, it will be from Pearl Harbor. They say we need to be packed and ready within the month," Donald answered.

"I ain't goin' to Hawaii," Linda stated emphatically. "Gina and I'll be here waiting for you when you get back."

Except for home with her parents, Barstow was all Linda knew, and the idea of being anywhere else with or without Donald wasn't a possibility in her mind.

Raising his voice, Donald said, "You can't stay here. I'm being transferred, so you won't have this house to live in."

"Then Gina and I will have to stay with momma and daddy," she said.

"No, you're both coming with me," Donald said.

On the verge of tears, Linda pleaded her case, pointing out how good things were going since she had been home.

"Please Donald, I ain't ready for this," Linda begged. The look on Donald's face should've been enough to convince her to stop talking, but she couldn't.

"Why, Donald?" Linda pleaded. "Tell me, why do we gotta go?" Staring at her, Donald said nothing.

Linda said, "If you won't let us to go stay with momma and daddy, then let me get a house off base here. I'll get a job to help pay for it," she said without considering what she'd do with Gina.

"Really? And who's going to take care of my daughter?" Donald asked.

"I don't know. I guess I'll get a babysitter, like you did," Linda said.

Knowing the second it came out of her mouth she shouldn't say it, but helpless to stop herself, Linda said, "I ain't going to Hawaii, Donald, and you can't make me."

Taking her by the shoulders, Donald said, "Oh, I can and I will. You're my wife and I won't leave you behind. You WILL go with me! And when I return, you will be in Hawaii waiting for me. Do you understand what I'm saying?" Donald asked.

The sound of Gina's scream drowned out the sound of Donald's demands. Shaking him off, Linda ran into the house. Gina was lying on the floor, apples and blood were everywhere.

"Good God in heaven, Gina Marie. What have you done now?" Linda screamed as Donald scooped Gina up into his arms, rushing her to the sink.

She watched franticly as Donald washed the blood off her little hand, trying to get the bleeding to stop, but the cut was too deep, and it wouldn't stop bleeding. So, with the kitchen towel wrapped around Gina's hand, they climbed in the car and headed for the hospital.

Fighting the memories of their last trip to the emergency room, Linda asked Gina, "How did this happen?"

Whimpering, Gina said, "Remember, you said I could have an apple."

"Yes, I remember, and I also remember telling you to do your puzzle and sit still," she said, reprimanding Gina.

"I know, but I wanted an apple, so I was bringing the bowl to you," Gina said.

"Gina Marie, why didn't you just bring me an apple?" Linda asked.

"I don't know," Gina answered, crying.

At the hospital, Donald explained what happened while Linda watched the doctor try to get the bleeding to stop.

Ignoring Donald, the doctor asked, "Gina, can you tell me what happened to your finger?"

"Momma said I could have an apple, but she forgot, so I took the apples to her," Gina said.

"Ouch!" Gina yelled as the doctor pulled back the skin.

"Where was your momma?" the doctor asked sweetly.

"She was on the front porch with my daddy," Gina said.

"So, you helped yourself, huh?" suggested the doctor.

With her head hung down, Gina answered, "Yes, sir."

"What were your momma and daddy doing?" the doctor asked.

"They were fighting," Gina answered.

Feeling uncomfortable with his questions, Linda said, "Excuse me, could you please just bandage her hand so I can take her home?"

"I wish I could, but I'm afraid it's impossible," the doctor answered.

"Impossible? Why?" Linda asked, looking frantically up at Donald. Donald placed his arm on her shoulder comfortingly, but Linda pushed his hand away.

The doctor explained the cut was deep and required stitches and asked them to please go to the waiting room.

Sitting in the waiting room, Linda reflected on the short three years of her daughter's life, feeling like a terrible momma.

"Donald, what if they take Gina away from us?" Linda asked.

"Why would you think something like that?" Donald asked angrily.

"Why shouldn't I?" Linda asked. "I ain't even sure I'm fit to be her momma. I can only imagine what the doctor is thinking. Remember, this is the same hospital Gina almost died in. I'm sure they have a record of it. You heard the questions he was askin'."

"I am aware of where we are. You don't need to remind me. This was just an accident, Linda. There's no need to blame yourself. You didn't hurt Gina," Donald whispered.

In her heart, Linda knew both instances were accidents. Knowing it didn't make it any easier. She couldn't help wondering how much more the poor child was going to have to endure with her as a momma.

* * *

Later, sitting on the floor next to Gina's bed, she watched her sleep. As the magnitude of the responsibility she carried for this tiny human washed over her, Linda whispered. "Gina Marie, Momma's sorry. It seems like I'm always doing somethin' wrong and you get hurt." Tears welled in her eyes. Brushing them away, Linda bowed her head, and prayed.

"Dear God, I need your help. I know I ain't been the best momma, but I'm tryin', and I promise I'll do better. Please, help me," she cried. "I can't go to Hawaii."

The following morning, she tried to reason with Donald again.

"Donald, please listen to me," she begged, but he refused. And his refusal had led to hers. She'd quit making his breakfast or packing his lunch. She and Gina ate before he got home so she didn't have to sit at the table with him and she slept on the couch every night. When she talked to him, it was only to beg him again. Each time he refused and finally Linda stopped talking to Donald altogether.

Desperate, she thought about leaving and taking Gina with her but deep down, she knew no matter how cruel Donald was being, it wasn't right to take Gina from him before he left for Vietnam.

Realizing nothing she said would change Donald's mind, Linda stopped talking and started packing.

One month to the day after Donald received his orders, they boarded the airplane for Hawaii. Linda was exhausted after spending half the night before talking to her momma. With her daddy already gone, her momma hadn't taken the news of Linda leaving very well. Crying, she begged Linda for hours, saying, "Please don't go, I need you here."

Terrified, but done trying to be happy and trying to love Donald, and although Linda didn't know how she was going to do it, she knew she had to leave him.

Well, she thought, *you've got thirteen months to figure it out.*

A few minutes later, she felt the airplane gently lift off and soon she was asleep.

Hawaii

From her window seat high above the island, Linda had to admit Hawaii was breathtakingly beautiful. The colors! The contrast between this world below her and the one she'd just left were vast.

The greens covering the hills were so lush, there were flowers of every color and miles of trees. The mountains appeared to have risen out of the ground, reaching great heights, then flattened out on top. Within the beautiful mixture of rock and foliage, she could see waterfalls. The turquoise blue water rolling up on golden beaches captivated her.

Looking over at Gina, sound asleep in Donald's lap, she gently shook her and whispered, "Gina, honey, we're here. Wake up. You don't wanna miss Hawaii from up here." Gina awoke with a squeal that certainly had awakened the entire airplane.

Once on the ground, in the back seat of their taxicab, they rode down wide streets lined with palm trees and again Linda felt in awe of the raw beauty.

The Pearl Harbor Naval base housing was nothing like Fort Irwin. The houses were bungalow style with a Polynesian flare, set back away from the street and surrounded by lush green lawns. The floor to ceiling windows had wooden shutters on each side. The houses were all painted the same white, but had high-pitched roofs painted in different colors. Theirs was red.

Taking a deep breath, Linda reached down to take Gina's hand and, as they walked up the path toward their new home, she said a prayer, hoping she'd find some peace here.

Although completely different on the outside, the inside of the house was the same: a small kitchen, a living room, two bedrooms, and a bathroom. Off the kitchen was a small backyard with a low fence. In the middle of the living room were the three boxes of the stuff they'd shipped ahead, mostly Gina's clothes and toys.

Moving the boxes into Gina's room, Linda and Donald worked side by side in silence, unpacking and putting away all the toys and clothes.

They left Gina playing quietly in her room and while they unpacked the rest of their meager belongings, Linda thought about the two children who'd married seven years ago and wondered what had happened to them. After everything they'd been through, they were still just barely more than strangers.

Concerned by the sudden silence in Gina's room, Linda tiptoed in and found her asleep in the middle of the floor, wrapped in her silk blanket. Smiling, she walked over to the bed and pulled back the covers, while Donald picked Gina up and laid her gently down on the bed.

The tiki torch-like streetlights cast a golden glow as the day turned to night. The activities of the day were catching up with Linda. Yawning, she walked out on the front porch and sat down in the Army issued chair and closed her eyes.

She heard the screen open and close and felt Donald's eyes upon her. Tired, she refused to open her eyes until she felt Donald's hand on her thigh. Then her eyes flew open.

Drawing her legs together, Linda hoped Donald would dare her to refuse him his rights. Like a good wife, she'd obeyed and come to Hawaii with him. That was where her being a good wife stopped. No longer intimidated, looking Donald square in the eye, she calmly said, "Please remove your hand."

Sighing, Donald removed his hand and sat down in the chair next to her, saying, "I hoped to stay here with you and Gina until I left for Vietnam, but I think you'd rather I leave now. Am I right?" he asked.

Linda did not know how to answer his question. The idea of Donald being gone and her not feeling the anger she felt every time she looked at him sounded wonderful. Then again, the idea of him leaving her all alone with Gina scared her to death.

While Linda wished Donald hadn't forced her to come to Hawaii, in all honesty, there was nothing for her stateside and Linda felt lost, like she didn't belong anywhere. Not in California, not with momma and daddy, and certainly not in here in Hawaii.

Taking her silence as an answer, Donald said, "I'll be staying in the barracks if you need to reach me."

"Donald, I am sorry," Linda said. "Please wait."

"Wait for what?" Donald asked. "Obviously, you couldn't care less if I stay or go," he stated coldly.

"No, you're wrong Donald." Linda said, "I care. For Gina's sake, I do care."

Donald hesitated, but said nothing. Then he turned and walked away. She watched until he disappeared around the corner before getting up and walking into the house. Disgusted with herself, Linda removed her clothing and climbed naked into bed, falling asleep immediately.

Sometime later, she woke up cold and moved closer to the middle of the bed, looking for her usual source of heat, but he was gone. Unable to fall back asleep, Linda got up and checked on Gina. Bending down to pull the covers up over her she noticed the tattered bandage on Gina's finger. The reality of being alone, thousands of miles away from family, with no husband and a three-year-old she'd already failed twice, felt like a ton of bricks on her shoulders. Falling to her knees beside Gina's bed in desperation, she closed her eyes and bowed her head, then lacking the strength to even pray, Linda climbed into bed with Gina and fell fast asleep.

* * *

She'd expected Donald to return the following day, but he didn't. When Gina asked where her daddy was, Linda answered, saying the only thing she knew to be true, "He's at work."

A week later, Linda was sitting at the table when she heard a knock on the front door. Instinctively, she knew it was Donald and that he'd come to tell her he was leaving.

Since Gina was napping, they spoke in whispers. Donald didn't stay long and when he left, he left her with a quick kiss on the cheek, an envelope telling her where he could be reached in an emergency and how to access money when she needed it.

It's so neat. So tidy. So simple, too simple. Shouldn't they have more to discuss than logistics and money? she thought.

Once again, Linda thought about begging Donald to send her and Gina home, but knowing it was pointless, she said nothing. Instead, she watched as he walked out, closing the door behind him.

* * *

On the day Donald's ship was set to sail, Linda got up early, bathed, dressed, and awakened her daughter. She put Gina in her favorite green dress and combed her hair into a ponytail. Then she called a cab.

Jumping up and down, Gina asked. "Where're we going, Momma?"

"We're goin' to say goodbye to your daddy," Linda answered.

"Why? Where's daddy going?" Gina asked.

Slipping into her leather loafers, Linda sat down on the edge of the couch, wondering how one went about telling an almost four-year-old child her daddy was off to fight a war. Saved by the blast of the cab horn, Linda and Gina were walking hand in hand down the path when Linda stopped mid-stride.

She couldn't believe what she saw. Parked next to the curb was her old beat-up Ford, the one with a broken taillight and a missing hubcap.

It was the most beautiful thing Linda had ever seen, and she choked back tears, remembering how she'd cursed Donald silently, thinking he'd sold it as just another way to control her existence from the other side of the world. Obviously, Donald hadn't sold her car, and Linda almost felt bad for the way she'd treated him.

* * *

The taxicab got Linda and Gina to the dock just as the USNS Weigel was raising her anchor. There were women and children everywhere, many openly crying, waving frantically toward the ship at the men lined up, leaning against the rails waving back just as frantically.

As she watched, Linda felt sorry Donald didn't know she and Gina were there. For her own sake and Gina's, she allowed her eyes to lock and hold on a man at the rear of the ship about Donald's height and weight. Waving excitedly, smiling bigger than she'd ever done in her life, Linda knelt down beside Gina, pointing up toward the ship and said, "Look Gina, there's daddy. Wave bye-bye to daddy."

Trying to block the sun out of her eyes, Gina said, "I don't see daddy,"

"Your daddy can see you sweetie, so just wave," Linda said.

"I can't see him," Gina said, concerned.

"It okay Gina, even though we can't see him, we know he's up there. So, let's wave so he'll see us," Linda suggested.

Gina waved as hard as she could, blowing kisses and said "Bye, daddy" over and over until finally, she buried her head in Linda's lap, crying.

As the crowd watched the ship pull away from the dock, Linda looked back at the crowd. It was as if she could read their minds and feel their fears, wondering if they'd ever see each other again. On the ship's bridge were thousands of husbands, fathers, sons, and brothers looking down upon their families. Linda recognized the looks on their faces, the same look she had seen on Donald's and ignored.

Why hadn't she considered Donald's fear? Was she really so cold and heartless? Linda took Gina's hand and walked back to the waiting taxicabs, disappointed in herself. As their cab drove away, Linda realized this wasn't only her and Gina's reality. It was the same for every single woman and child standing on the dock. They were all here alone, none of them knowing what their futures held.

* * *

After tucking her sleeping daughter into bed, Linda stood in the middle of the dark living room with her purse in hand, wondering what now? Feeling overly warm, she walked over to the tall window and pulled on the heavy cord, opening the blind. Hoping for a cool breeze, she pushed it open. Standing back, she allowed her eyes to adjust to the light. Looking around, as if seeing the place for the first time, she noticed furniture both bright and colorful. The walls were stark white, heavily textured, and adorned with pictures of beautiful tropical places. Pretty rugs spread across the tile floors in several places. The tall windows on either side of the front door were covered by slatted blinds.

It all seems so neat and pretty. Too neat and pretty. What a farce. The military takes our husbands and leaves us here alone, living in pretty little boxes while we wait for a phone call or a letter. Well, I ain't gonna wait around to see if Donald comes back or not, she thought.

Standing it in the middle of the room holding her purse, she looked at the door, wondering if she had the courage to walk out of it.

Then she remembered the car. She walked out the door. Opening the door of the car, she sat down in driver's seat. The familiar scent of the car, of Donald, her own perfume and of home overwhelmed her. Reaching over, she opened the glove box, praying she'd find the keys. What she found was a large envelope and a carton of cigarettes.

Her hands shook as she opened the envelope. Inside, she found a silver key and a folded piece of paper. Linda addressed the little silver key first. Taking a deep breath, she slipping it into the ignition. Then she lit a cigarette, unfolded the note, and read:

My Dearest Linda,

Please forgive me for leaving you and Gina in Hawaii like this. It hurt me making you come here against your will, but it was the only way I could be sure you'd be here when I return. You and Gina are all I have, and I can't lose you. These past few years have been hell. I know I've played my part in it too and for that, I'm sorry. I hope someday you will forgive me.

When I come home, if I come home, I pray you'll give me a second chance.

Love, Donald

P.S. I felt the least I could do was to give you wheels. Enjoy the Island.

Dropping the note as if burnt, she turned on the ignition. Putting the car in gear, she let her foot off the brake, pulling away from the curb. Despite the immediate sense of liberation, Linda had only gone a few feet when she slammed on the brakes. Turning off the ignition, she smiled, remembering Donald's closing words, *enjoy the island*. She may be alone and in a strange place, but with a car, the possibilities were endless. Yes, enjoying the island was just what she and Gina were going to do.

* * *

Settling into a routine, each day, Linda and Gina walked to the park hand in hand so Gina could play with the other children. Being a social child, Gina quickly made friends with Sarah, the little girl next door. The two were inseparable, and soon so were their mothers.

Being one of the few wives lucky enough to have a car, Linda made many friends, too. She spent most of her days driving one or two of her new friends from place to place, but since she was happiest behind the wheel of a car, she didn't mind.

One night, sitting on the porch after putting Sarah and Gina to bed, Sarah's mother Jan asked, "Hey Linda, would you like a beer?"

"I don't know, I guess it's okay, but I like Coke better," Linda answered. "Why?"

"I didn't ask if you liked beer," Jan said. "I asked if you wanted one."

"Do you have some?" Linda asked.

Smiling, Jan answered, "No, but we could go buy some."

"And where are we gonna buy beer?" Linda asked.

"I guess since the commissary is already closed, we'd have to go off base, but you have a car," Jan said.

"Yes, I do, but I ain't goin' alone. And what about the kids?" Linda asked.

"They're asleep and we won't be long," was Jan's answer.

The idea was both exciting and scary. She'd never left Gina alone before. She felt nervous and her heart raced. "Okay, I'm game but let's hurry," she said.

Approaching the front gate, Linda felt like a schoolgirl again sneaking out of her daddy's house. She slowed the car down, certain they'd be stopped and questioned. As the military police waved them on and, just like that, they were off the base.

The adrenaline surging through her veins was intoxicating. Linda didn't need beer. What she needed was just miles and miles of open road in front of her.

She hadn't expected freedom to feel this good. All she could think of was driving as fast as she could, as far as she could, with the windows rolled down. Wind in her face and the country radio station blaring.

Walking into the liquor store, Linda felt like a kid who'd just stolen cookies from the kitchen when her momma wasn't looking. The enormous man behind the counter didn't seem to care why they were out after dark or where their children were. Maybe because he didn't know they were being naughty, but Linda did.

A naughty wife whose husband was too far away to know what she was up to. A naughty momma, whose daughter was at home, asleep and alone.

Being naughty felt amazing, and Linda wasn't ready for it to end. Leaving the parking lot, instead of turning left, she turned right.

Concerned, Jan said, "Hey, you turned the wrong way."

Laughing, Linda said, "I know. I just ain't ready for this ride to end yet."

* * *

Back home, with a six-pack of beer and enough cigarettes to last for a week, Linda and Jan sat on the porch laughing, reliving their adventure.

"I was so nervous," Linda said, giggling. "I can't wait to do it again."

"Me either, but let's keep this to ourselves," Jan said. "I don't think the other wives would approve,"

Opening a beer can and handing it to Jan, Linda said, "I couldn't care less what they think. We can do whatever we wanna do."

"I wish that were true, Linda," Jan said with a deep sigh.

And the more they talked about what they couldn't do, the madder they got and the more they drank. And the more they drank, the louder they got.

"Shouldn't we be able to? Linda asked.

"Sure, we should, but let's face it, this is a man's world," Jan answered.

"Let me ask you something? If you could do anything you wanted to, what would you do?" Jan asked.

While Linda thought about Jan's question, Jan said, "I know what I'd do. I'd start by getting a job so I could afford a divorce."

Linda nodded in agreement, then said, "I think I'll go in now; the beers made me sleepy."

Locking the door behind her, she went to bed, thinking about Jan's question. What would she do if she were free to make her own decisions? What would it be like to work? To earn her own money and make her own way? Why should she have to stay home and be a wife and have babies just because that's what her momma did?

Linda tossed and turned, lamenting the unfairness of it all until eventually the beer won the argument and she slept soundly.

* * *

It seemed like only a few minutes later when she woke to the sound of Jan's voice calling her name over and over. Waking up, she realized Jan was in her bedroom. Confused, Linda asked, "How'd you get in here?"

"The door was unlocked," Jan said.

"That's not possible. I always lock the door," she answered. Then sheer panic hit, "Where's Gina?" Linda asked.

"It's okay, Gina is fine. She's in the living room. When I went out to walk the dogs this morning, I found her sitting on the porch," Jan explained.

"Is she alright?" Linda asked, slipping into her robe.

"Yes, she seems fine. She was cold, so I wrapped her in a blanket. She's on the couch watching television," Jan answered.

Walking Jan to the door, Linda saw one of the dining room chairs was next to the door. She thanked Jan for bringing Gina home.

Closing the door, she took a deep breath and yelled, "Gina Marie, what in God's name were you thinking?"

"I'm sorry, Momma," Gina said, instantly crying hysterically.

Linda screamed a barrage of questions at Gina, which only made her cry harder. Not knowing what else to do, Linda scooped Gina up and carried her to her bedroom, tossing her none to gently on her bed, then turned and walked out, slamming the door behind her.

She was on the couch wondering what she was going to do with her child when Gina came out of her room, dragging her silk blanket. Climbing up on the couch, Gina said, "I'm sorry, Momma, but I couldn't find you."

"What do you mean you couldn't find me? I was in my bed," Linda said.

"No, you weren't. I woke up scared and went looking for you," Gina argued.

Wondering if Gina had actually woken up while she and Jan were gone, Linda said, "Gina, Momma needs you to understand what you did was very bad. I've told you over and over you're never to leave this house without me."

"Where were you? I couldn't find you," Gina asked.

Sticking with her story, Linda said, "I told you I was in my bed. You must've been dreaming."

Relieved she didn't have to answer any more questions because Gina had fallen asleep and grateful nothing bad happened, Linda promised herself it wouldn't happen again.

* * *

A few weeks later though, when Jan said, "I think we need another night out."

Linda said "That sounds like fun. What should we do?"

"I've heard of a place called the Tiki Room. It's a nightclub off base," Jan said. "I could get a babysitter for the kids and we could get dressed up and go out. What do you think?"

"I don't know about a nightclub," Linda said. "How about a movie with the kids?"

"How about we take a drive and go check it out?" Jan whispered.

"Now?" Linda asked.

"Yes, now. We won't go in. We'll just drive by and look," Jan answered.

"No Jan, I don't think so," Linda said. "When I think of what could've happened last time, no," she said, "I just can't."

When Jan persisted, Linda gave in. And for the second time, they tiptoed down the path, leaving Gina and Jan's kids sleeping at home alone.

* * *

The Tiki Room nightclub was in a dark wood building in the middle of a lush resort area just off the base. Tiki torches sparkled on either side of the door.

Cute little huts surrounded it, with winding paths leading from one hut to the other. In the courtyard, to the left side of the club was a waterfall with multicolored lighting that colored the water running over large lava rocks. From the dimly lit parking lot, Linda and Jan sat in the car with the windows rolled down, watching as a well-dressed couple walked up to the doors of the club. The gentleman opened the door, bowing slightly to the lady, allowing her to go in first, then walked in behind her. Linda could hear the music playing.

"Sounds fun, huh?" Jan said.

"We better head back," Linda said. "We've been gone long enough."

"Okay," Jan said, "I agree but what do you think? Should I find a babysitter for next weekend?"

Linda's heart raced, and in what sounded like someone else's voice, she answered, "It sounds like fun. Okay, why the hell not? Call the sitter."

Joe

On Friday night, after leaving the kids with the babysitter, Jan and Linda walked up to the front door of the Tiki Room. Remembering how the gentlemen held the door open for the lady, Linda opened the door wide. Bowing slightly, Linda allowed Jan to walk in first, laughing at her own silly antics.

They claimed the last two seats at the far end of the bar. On the opposite side of the bar, a dark-skinned man with enormous arms smiled at them.

"Good evening, ladies. Welcome to the Tiki room. May I have the pleasure of your names?" he asked.

"I'm Linda and this is my friend, Jan. What's your name?"

With a hearty laugh Linda liked immediately, the bartender answered, "My name is Joe. What can I get you ladies to drink?"

"We'll have beer, Joe," Linda said.

"What kind of beer? We have several," Joe said.

Not wanting to admit this was her first time in a bar, Linda smiling, saying, "I don't know, Joe. Surprise me."

Chatting across the bar, Linda learned Joe was born and raised on Oahu and had never been off the Island. During the day, he worked odd jobs and at night he tended bar at the Tiki Room to feed his wife and six children. He wasn't overly handsome, but what he lacked in looks he made up for in charm. There was an instant chemistry between Linda and Joe. Joe felt it, Linda felt it, even Jan felt it.

On the ride home, Jan was unusually quiet and when Linda asked why, she said, "I don't think we should go back there."

"Why, I enjoyed myself. Didn't you?" Linda asked.

"Yes, I did, but I saw the way you and Joe were looking at each other. He's married and so are you. I've got a bad feeling about this," Jan said.

Laughing, Linda said, "Hey, wait a minute. You were the one who said we should go out. And now I've made a friend, and it's a bad thing?"

"I don't know. Maybe," Jan answered.

Deep-down Linda knew Jan was probably right. However, she also knew as soon as she could, she'd be going back to the Tiki Room. Back to see Joe.

Two weeks later, Linda was antsy. She'd thought of nothing else since the night they met, but purposely hadn't mentioned Joe or the Tiki Room to Jan.

"Hey Jan," Linda asked, "do you think we can get a sitter again on Friday?"

"I can try. Why? Where do you want to go?" Jan asked.

Linda's eyes lit up like fireflies when she said, "To the Tiki Room!"

"Seriously Linda. Do you think that's a good idea?" Jan asked.

"Yes, I do," Linda answered. "Our lives are the same, day in and day out-kids, kids, and more kids. We deserve a night out."

"I agree. We deserve a night out but, let's be honest, Linda, you just want to see Joe again," Jan said.

"You're right, I do," Linda admitted. "I like him. He makes me laugh. Is there something wrong with that?" she asked.

"I guess not. Okay, let me see what I can do," Jan said, walking out the door.

While Jan was gone, Linda checked her mail. Finding yet another letter from Donald, she tossed it on the table with his other unopened letters and went out to check on Gina and Sarah, playing in the yard.

Oh, how she longed for the days when she'd run to the mailbox hoping for a letter from Donald. Now, she didn't care what he had to say. As long as she received his letters, she knew he was alive and, for now, that was all she needed to know.

She was still trying to deal with the anger of being dumped here. The car had helped, at first. Then after driving from one side of the island to the other, several times, now trapped was all she felt.

When she walked back into the house, Jan was holding Donald's letters in her hand. "Aren't you going to read these?" she asked.

Opening a Coke and handing it to Jan, Linda answered, "Nope."

"I can't believe you aren't going to read those letters," Jan said.

"Believe it," she said, and having no intention of spending the afternoon talking about the letters or their husbands, Linda asked, "Hey, were you able to get a sitter?"

Raising her Coke up in the air, Jan smiled, saying, "Here's to Friday night."

* * *

On Friday night, dressed in her prettiest pink dress, Linda drove off base with Jan and headed straight to the Tiki Room. When they arrived, Joe wasn't behind the bar. Disappointed, but determined not to let it show, she ordered two beers at the bar, found a small table in the front of the dance floor, and sat down.

A few minutes later, another big Hawaiian man with beautiful brown skin and a pleasant smile showed up with their beers.

"Good evening. I think these belong to you," the bartender said.

"Thank you," Linda said. Then sweetly asked, "Where's Joe tonight?"

Producing a huge smile, the bartender said, "It's Joe's night off. My name is Cane and I promise to take good care of you."

"Is your name really Cain? Like Cain in the Bible?" Linda asked.

With another big smile, Cane said, "No, Cane, like the sweet island sugar cane."

Smiling at Jan, Linda said, "Oh, he is cute."

"Since Joe isn't here, do you even want to stay?" Jan asked.

"Of course I do. Why wouldn't I?" Linda asked.

"You and I both know you came here to see Joe, and I still think you're messing with fire, if you ask me."

"Well, I'm a big girl, Jan, and nobody asked you." Then, raising her beer, Linda said, "Here's to the big girls in this world."

Linda did not know how much time passed before Joe walked into the club, but she knew the second he did. Smiling ear to ear, she stopped dancing, rooted to her spot on the dance floor, as their eyes locked.

Jan grabbed Linda's arm, leading her off the dance floor, saying, "Linda, I really think we should leave now."

Never taking her eyes off Joe, Linda said, "I appreciate your concern, Jan, but I know what I want, adding, I want another beer."

She ordered two beers at the bar, then turned, and walked toward Joe.

As Linda approached him, Joe opened his arms, and she walked into them. As his arms closed around her, Linda closed her eyes, feeling safer than she'd felt in perhaps her entire life, and she wished the embrace to never end. Knowing people were watching, she pulled away.

They talked, laughed, and drank until finally Jan said, "Linda, the babysitter needs to be home by twelve. We have to leave."

Never taking her eyes off Joe, Linda answered. "The keys are in my purse. You go ahead, Joe will give me a ride home."

"What would I tell Gina? No, I think you should come now," Jan said.

Knowing Jan was right, Linda asked, "Can you give us a few minutes?"

"Yes, I'll be waiting in the car, but hurry," Jan answered.

"We won't be long, I promise," she said. And she wasn't.

* * *

When they got to Jan's home, Gina was sound asleep.

"Just leave her sleeping," Jan said.

Nodding, Linda hugged Jan and thanked her.

Back in her own bungalow with the windows open and the breeze blowing in off the ocean, Linda undressed and slipped between the sheets completely naked. Sliding in on her belly, she allowed herself to experience the feel of the sheets against her naked flesh. She laid there unmoving, face down, until the evening breezes turned cold. As she pulled the cotton blanket up over her, her hand brushed lightly across her nipple and the explosion between her thighs was delightful.

* * *

Two weeks later, Linda saw Joe again. After dropping Gina off at daycare, she drove to the secluded beach where they had agreed to meet. When she arrived, Joe wasn't there and for a split second, she considered leaving. The thought of being alone with him scared her, but it also made her body tingle all over with excitement.

When Joe arrived, a nervous Linda jumped out of her car and ran toward the beach. Laughing, Joe ran and easily caught up with her. Then he pulled her down onto the sand. Knowing their time together was short drove their passion.

Linda could barely breathe as Joe kissed her long and hard, thrusting his tongue inside her mouth. His hands were everywhere, and she wanted them there. Then, with a boldness she'd never known, Linda raised her dress up over her head, tossing it aside. She prayed Joe would take her quickly and none too gently, but he just laughed, whispering in his native tongue something she couldn't understand, which fueled her passion even more.

With the smell of the nearby plumeria filling the air, Linda longed to feel Joe on top of her. She arched her back, desperate for what only Joe could give her. Joe was in no hurry.

The feel of his manhood against her leg left her breathless, and Linda wrapped her arms around his neck, rubbing herself against him even harder. Her head spun, and her heart pounded as Joe kissed her again and again. Tenderly stroking her hair, he said, "Patience, my little Hokeo, patience."

* * *

Joe and Linda were together whenever it was possible. Being a day laborer, there were days he wasn't called to work, and they'd spend every minute together.

Linda signed Gina up for preschool and when Joe wasn't working, she'd drop her off, pick Joe up and off they'd go. Sometimes they'd pick up food and beer and find a secluded spot to be alone.

Other times, the need to touch each other was more than either of them could bare, and they'd drive to a secluded place, park, and fondle until neither of them could breathe but each time Joe held back saying "Patience, my little Hokeo, patience."

In his distinct island slang, Joe flattered her, telling her she was beautiful. He never called her by her given name, only by the name he'd given her, Hokeo.

She didn't know what Hokeo meant, and she didn't care. She loved the sound of the word as it rolled off his tongue, and hoped it meant he loved her.

Joe was unlike anyone she'd ever met. He wasn't only funny, but fun. And when he laughed, he laughed from way down deep in his belly. It was loud and infectious, and made Linda laugh like she'd never laughed before.

With Joe, Linda learned she could be happy, and she didn't take herself so seriously. With each laugh, her fears melted away, and she wanted nothing more than to laugh and be happy with Joe forever.

They both knew what was happening between them was wrong, and neither cared.

For weeks, Linda and Joe fought their desires for each other, not allowing their passions to go further than fondling. Just knowing one day they would make love was enough for now.

The news of Joe and Linda spread. Linda didn't know how, but she suspected it was Jan. And Jan was right. The other wives would have nothing to do with her, car or not. Their opinion of her didn't bother Linda in the least. She was happy for the first time in her life, and that was what mattered.

* * *

Then finally the day came they'd both waited for. Sitting on the side of a dirt road in Linda's car, wrapped in each other's arms, Joe whispered, "Hokeo, I cannot wait any longer. Please let me make love to you."

She felt her answer first in her heart, then in her soul, but barely heard her answer because the blood rushing through her veins was so loud. Her body tingled from head to toe, and the thought of waiting another minute was almost more than she could bear.

"Yes Joe," Linda pleaded. "Please, make love to me."

"Not here, though. I know a place. Move over, he said. I'll drive."

They drove to the most beautiful place Linda had ever seen in her life—a plateau high above the ocean, surrounded by luscious green ferns. The grass was soft and felt cool to her bare feet. A true paradise. Their own garden of Eden.

As they kissed and caressed, Joe whispered, "Hokeo, your skin is the softest I've ever felt. I cannot wait to make you mine."

Linda inhaled his words as if they were oxygen. Like music, they touched her soul, and they gently wooed her heart until she was sure she was about to faint. Melting into Joe's arms, she closed her eyes, surrendering all. Then she gasped in shock as he picked her up and laid her down.

The grass was cool beneath her. In contrast, Joe's large, rugged hands were hot upon her skin as he unbuttoned her blouse, pushing it aside to kiss her neck.

She could smell his sweet breath as he kissed her mouth. Using his tongue, he traced a line over her chin, down her neck, stopping just between her breasts.

Standing up, Linda slowly removed all her clothing, then returned to their bed of grass and waited as Joe did the same.

Naked, he returned to her, kissing one shoulder, then the other. She trembled once again as his warm wet tongue ran downward between her now fully exposed breasts. With her eyes closed, Linda lay breathlessly awaiting Joe's next move. Then her eyes flew open as Joe's hand closed completely over her breast. Her mind was screaming NO, but her body was screaming YES as his tongue brushed across her nipple.

Scared but sure if she waited a second longer she would die on-the-spot, Linda whispered, "Now, Joe. Now!"

It was as if God had created them for this moment. They rose and fell together. Every second was better than the one before. And with each move, Joe took Linda to heights she'd never experienced.

Linda let her eyes flutter open for a split second. Looking up toward the heavens in silent prayer, she both thanked God for this moment and asked for His forgiveness.

* * *

From that day, there was something unleashed in Linda that she couldn't control. She simply had to be in Joe's arms and the days when she wasn't were physically painful.

Gina had become a burden and Linda looked for any reason to leave her behind to find fulfillment in Joe's arms.

Jan tried to voice her concerns, but Linda wouldn't listen to them. She was beyond happy and knew where she wanted to be for the rest of her life. Wrapped in Joe's arms, safe and loved. When they were together, Linda didn't hide the fact she was in love with Joe. In fact, she told him every chance she got. And she knew Joe loved her too, even though he hadn't said so.

Linda never lied to herself about the reality of their situation. She knew Joe was married with children and so was she. She also knew it was something they'd have to face one day, but for now, she refused to think about it.

When they were together, they spent their time either in morning interludes in a cottage at the resort or in their own private paradise, high on the plateau, where they'd strip each other wildly and make love with complete abandon.

Her favorites were the nights Joe knocked softly on her back door and they quietly tiptoed to her bedroom, where they'd make love soft and slow until she fell asleep in his arms. And when she woke up, he would be gone.

She didn't know how he got on or off the base, and she didn't care. When he was with her, he didn't speak of his wife or his life away from her and Linda didn't ask. She knew very little about him, really, but that didn't matter either. She loved him with her entire being. He was the reason she got up in the morning and the reason she slept at night. And he was all she thought about during the hours in between.

Trouble In Paradise

Linda knew she couldn't live without their love and her current existence. Without Joe, there was no life. Their blissful days together turned into blissful weeks, then months. By the end of the third blissful month, Linda was certain she was pregnant, but she made a doctor's appointment to make sure.

In the doctor's office waiting to be called, Linda couldn't stop smiling. She knew she should be worried or even ashamed, but she wasn't. How could she be ashamed of what they'd created in love?

Closing the door behind her a few minutes later, the nurse asked, "What brings you in today, Mrs. Holloway?"

Beaming, Linda answered, "My monthly is late."

"Then we should get a urine sample to see if you're pregnant," she said.

As the room got hot and felt smaller, Linda was dizzy and sick to her stomach. she cursed herself for even coming. There was no need for a doctor to tell her she was pregnant. She knew.

It had been so difficult to conceive Gina, Linda never once considered the possibility she might get pregnant. Or maybe deep down she didn't care. Either way, she was pregnant, and she was ecstatic.

* * *

Within the hour, Linda left the doctor's office smiling from ear to ear with lab slips, prenatal vitamins, and confirmation she was two months pregnant. She picked up Gina at preschool and, in silent celebration, took her out to lunch.

While Gina ate her burger and fries, Linda thought about at least a dozen different ways she could tell Joe, never once considering he might not be happy about the pregnancy. Obviously, he liked kids. After all, he had six of them already.

She realized her pregnancy complicated things even more. And although she'd never asked Joe if he'd leave his wife for her, she felt deep in her heart he would.

For the first time in her life, everything felt right, and Linda had no doubts. It's the little things, the way her hand fit into his, how they could talk for hours about nothing and how Joe seemed to know what she needed without her even asking. When they were together, time didn't exist. Donald, Gina, Joe's wife and his kids didn't exist. And now she was having his baby. Yes, for the first time, everything felt right.

Excited, Linda needed to tell someone about the baby and what better someone than its father? With no one to watch Gina, she dressed her in a pretty white organdy dress with pink roses embroidered on the collar and white sandals.

Twirling around to watch the bottom of her dress flare out, Gina asked, "Where are we going all dressed up, Momma?"

Linda answered simply, "I need to talk to a friend, so we're goin' for a ride. Afterward, if you're good, we'll get milkshakes."

Praying Gina wouldn't ask any more questions, Linda said, "Now go sit on the couch and try not to mess yourself up while I get ready."

She chose a white sleeveless dress with bold pink flowers and white leather loafers for herself. She brushed her teeth, ran a comb through her hair, and put on lipstick, trying not to think about the task at hand. As ready as she would ever be, Linda bowed her head, said a silent prayer, and walked into the living room to find Gina.

"Momma, look who's here," Gina said.

Linda froze in mid-stride. The front door was wide open and on the other side was Jan, holding Sarah's hand.

"Momma, can Sarah and I play outside?" Gina asked.

Linda had seen little of Jan since her relationship with Joe began. Her disappointed looks were the last thing Linda needed. So, she'd purposely gone out of the way to avoid them. Holding tight to Gina's hand, Linda smiled, saying, "Hi Jan. We were just on our way out. Is everything okay?"

"Yes, everything is fine. We've just missed you. Where are you two off to?" Jan asked.

Ignoring Jan's question all together, Linda walked out the door, pulling it closed behind her, saying, "Okay Gina, say goodbye to Sarah. We've gotta go now. "I'm sorry Jan," Linda said. "I am running late, but let's get together soon."

In the car, Gina asked, "Where are we goin' again, Momma?"

"Remember, we're goin' for a ride to see my friend," Linda answered.

"What friend? What's her name? Do I know her?" Gina asked.

She knew taking Gina was going to be awkward and thought about turning back, but she couldn't wait. "No, this is a new friend. His name is Joe," Linda answered.

* * *

When Linda walked into the bar, clinging to Gina's hand, Joe saw her right away and she heard him say, "Back in ten."

Linda smiled at him. Joe didn't smile back. Outside, he turned to look at her, and the look on his face was anything but happy. Thinking it was because of Gina, Linda said, "Gina, how about you go over yonder and look at the pretty flowers? Momma will be over there in a few minutes." Gina didn't move.

Not taking her eyes off Joe, Gina asked, "Momma, who is that man?"

Pushing Gina gently toward the flower bed, Linda answered, "It's a friend and I need to talk to him. Run along now and see the pretty flowers, like I said."

"Okay, but hurry 'cause I want to go play with Sarah," Gina said.

As Gina walked away, Joe asked, "What's up, Hokeo? It must be important if you brought your kid with you."

Beaming, Linda smiled up at Joe and said, "I just found out I'm pregnant and I couldn't wait to tell you."

Joe's silence was the hardest thing Linda had ever encountered. Then the look on his face changed from shock to sadness.

Linda was beginning to worry, wondering why Joe hadn't said anything, then she realized his silence was saying everything.

As the tears welled up in her eyes, threatening to spill, Joe said, "Hokeo, I don't know what to say to you. You know I care deeply for you, but I am married and so are you. One day, your husband will return from the war, and you will leave me. I've always known that, and I thought you did, too."

"I know, but now I don't gotta leave," Linda said. "I can stay here in Hawaii. Gina can start school in Hawaii and our baby will be born here."

The more she spoke, the clearer the future looked, and it all made perfect sense.

"No," Joe said, adamantly. "You can't stay here. You do not belong here. When your husband returns, you must go home with him."

With tears running down her cheeks, Linda asked, "How can I go home with him? I don't love him. I love you."

"Hokeo," Joe said, reaching for her hand. "As much as I care for you, this was never going to be more than what it has been."

"Maybe not for you, but it's been everything to me. I love you and I will leave my husband because I don't love him," Linda said.

With tears in his eyes, Joe said, "Hokeo, you must understand. I will never leave the mother of my children."

Bored with the flowers, Gina ran up, asking, "Momma, can we go home now?"

Looking down at Gina, Linda said, "Okay, in a few minutes, first I need to finish talkin' to my friend." When Linda looked up, Joe was already gone. And so was her reason for living.

"Who was that man, Momma?" Gina asked.

"He's just a friend," Linda answered. "A friend I won't be seeing again," she said as she took Gina's hand.

"Is he why you're crying?" Gina asked.

Wiping the tears away, Linda smiled and said, "I am fine. Let's go home."

Deep down, Linda knew she was anything but fine, but right now she needed to hold herself together, for Gina's sake.

"Good. Can we go for milkshakes now?" Gina asked.

While Gina drank her milkshake, Linda smoked cigarette after cigarette, very much aware that, except for Gina and the baby on the way, now she really was all alone. No family, no friends, no Joe, and probably no Donald.

In a moment's time, her reality had shifted. Now if Donald came home, he'd come home to a wife who'd have given birth to another man's baby. And she was certain he'd divorce her.

* * *

As they walked up the path, she saw Jan and Sarah walking toward them.

Seeing Linda's face, Jan asked, "Have you been crying?"

Linda shook her head no, then said to Gina, "You better run and get changed if you're gonna go play with Sarah."

As Gina and Sarah ran off ahead of them, Jan said, "I can see something's wrong. Do you want to talk about it?" she asked. Then, before Linda could answer, Jan said, "Dear God, it's Donald, isn't it?"

"No, it's not Donald. As far as I know, he's okay," Linda assured her.

"Then is it about Joe?" Jan asked.

Linda didn't answer Jan's question. Instead, she asked for a favor. "Jan, would you mind if the girls played at your house?" Linda asked. "I've got a terrible headache and I need to lie down."

"Sure, just call when you wake up and I'll bring Gina home," Jan said.

"Thank you," Linda said, just as Gina, wearing her play clothes and carrying her sandals, came running out yelling, "I'm ready!" Forcing a smile, Linda waved goodbye to Gina before walking into the house and closing the door.

Despite the muggy weather, she was shivering. Finally alone, Linda allowed the heart wrenching pain to come forth, and it came in a mournful wail, as she fell to the floor. From the depths of her soul, Linda cried. Her heart broke into a million pieces as she lay on the hard, cold surface.

The pain was so intense Linda felt sure she was going to die from it. Rolled up in a fetal position, she rocked herself back and forth, until finally exhausted, she slept.

When she woke up, the house was dark, and her head pounded. Turning on a light, Linda lit a cigarette and called Jan.

"The girls are fine and having fun. How about I keep Gina tonight?" Jan suggested. Linda agreed and was about to hang up when Jan said, "Hey, I'm worried about you. You know I'm here if you need to talk."

"Thank you, but I am sorry I can't," Linda said, hanging up without saying goodbye.

The warm evening breeze carried the sounds of the night through her open bedroom window. She tried not to think of Joe, but how could she not? He'd been all she'd thought about for months, every waking moment, one thought after another about Joe. In the darkness, her mind played cruel games with her.

First, asking how you could've been so stupid, thinking Joe loved you. When Linda argued saying she knew Joe loved her, her mind called her a fool, saying he'd used her, and was laughing at her now.

Linda got up and walked into the front room. Talking to herself out loud, she said, "You can't blame Joe for this. This here is all your doin'. Jan tried to warn you, but no, you wouldn't listen', sayin' you were a big girl and knew what you were doin'. And now, missy, you've got no one to blame except yourself."

Linda walked into the bathroom, opened the medicine chest and was looking for the aspirin, when she saw the bottle of sleeping pills Dr. Hall prescribed for her months ago.

She picked up the bottle and closed the medicine chest. She slowly walked back to her bedroom, sat down on the edge of the bed, and placed the bottle of pills on the nightstand.

It seemed like years since the last time she'd really prayed. Not knowing what else to do, with tears streaming down her face, Linda looked up toward the ceiling, closed her eyes and prayed out loud, asking, "Dear God, what I'm I gonna do?"

With her eyes closed, Linda let her mind wander. What she wouldn't give right now to hear his gentle tap on her back door. She imagined opening the door and Joe taking her in his arms, begging for her forgiveness, telling her he'd been wrong and all he wanted was her and their baby.

The thought of never seeing Joe again, never being held in his arms or hearing his silky voice calling her Hokeo, was unbearable.

How was she supposed to face Donald, her family? Dear God, how was she supposed to face tomorrow?

Sitting up straight, drying her eyes, she reached for the bottle. There was only one way to end this unbearable pain. Opening the bottle, she emptied the contents into her hand. She raised her hand and looked at the pills, fully aware they had the power to take away her pain, to end the fear of facing it all.

Then she remembered Gina and her unborn baby. Cold and numb, Linda dropped the pills on the floor, crawled back into bed, and pulled the covers up over her head. Clutching her belly, she cried herself to sleep.

* * *

The next few months passed slowly. She took Gina out of preschool and, unless they needed food or there was a doctor's appointment, they rarely left the house. There wasn't anywhere she wanted to go and certainly no one she cared to see. Jan tried several times to reach out, but Linda had no interest in seeing the *I told you so* look on Jan's face. She spent her days locked in her bungalow, watching her belly grow, knowing the hardest part of her life lay ahead of her.

She wasn't afraid. She believed God would see her through it, protecting both her and her baby, and even though she wouldn't have Joe, she'd always have his baby.

* * *

This pregnancy was nothing like her first. Most days she was so tired she couldn't hold her eyes open. She moved the television from the living room to the bedroom so Gina could watch cartoons and be in the same room while Linda slept.

Thoughts of Joe crept into her mind, and she didn't fight them. She knew deep down there wouldn't be a day in her life that she didn't think of Joe and of her time in Hawaii, and she was fine with that.

However, she wondered, if the saying time heals all wounds was true, how long it took. Because so far, her heart wasn't healing.

* * *

In December, the weather changed, and the days got cooler. With light winds and no humidity, it reminded Linda of home. While Joe was in her life, Linda hadn't even thought of home or her momma. Just like she had with Donald's letters, Linda avoided her momma's calls and letters until eventually they both stopped. Eventually Jan stopped coming around, too.

So, when a knock on the front door came, it startled her. She opened the door and blinked into the sun, unable to see who it was. She put her hand up over her eyes and her voice shook as she asked, "Can I help you?"

As her eyes adjusted to the light, Linda saw a tall man in Navy service dress whites. His cap was under his arm and his hand held a large white envelope. "I'm looking for Linda Holloway. Are you Mrs. Holloway?" he asked.

"Yes, I am," she answered as her hand slid to her belly.

The tall man said nothing else. Handing her the envelope, he tipped his cap, turned, and walked away. She knew the contents of the envelope could only mean one of two things. Either Donald was dead, or he was coming home, and she wondered which one would be worse.

Sitting down on the couch, Linda placed the envelope down on the coffee table and lit a cigarette. Common sense told her if Donald was dead, they wouldn't tell her like this. Not with just a cold white envelope. Her hands shook as she turned the envelope over, unfastening the metal clip.

Jumping up on the couch next to her, Gina asked, "What is it, Momma?"

"I ain't sure, but I think it might be a letter from your daddy," she said.

Inside the big envelope was a smaller envelope and, opening it, she confirmed it was a letter from Donald. Silently, she read it to herself.

My Dearest Linda,

Please forgive me for delivering this letter to you this way. It wasn't my intention to scare you, but I had to be sure you received it.

He had scared her, yes, but considering all his letters were unopened and unanswered, Linda understood Donald's need to know she'd received this one, so she read on.

The months here have been pure hell on earth. So much has happened here, some of which I could never explain.

If you've listened to the news or read any of my letters, you'll understand what I've endured here in Vietnam. I have a deep-seated hate for all that has transpired, but it is behind me now and I'm coming home.

I've missed you and Gina so much and I know you were mad at me for making you go to Hawaii, but I hope by now you've come to terms with it and realized it was for the best.

She laughed, as if she could come to terms with it. No, I'll never forgive him for making me come here. Rubbing her enormous belly, she knew she would never be sorry either. How could she be?

I am looking forward to getting home, settling down and increasing our family. I'm sure Gina will love having a baby brother or sister to play with.
Anyway, I'll write again soon when I have a definite date.
Yours truly,
Donald

Linda read Donald's letter over and over, thinking of Joe. She knew they would never be together, but entertained the possibility of her and Gina staying in Hawaii. She'd saved some of her allotted money and with it, she could rent a small house on the island. After the baby was born, she could get a job. Her heart raced with excitement at the mere thought of it. Gina could start school on the island and her baby would grow up here in Hawaii, maybe not knowing her father, but at least being near him. She could raise the kids here alone. She didn't need Donald, Linda told herself.

Then reality hit. Who was she kidding? Stroking the blond head of her sleeping daughter. Donald would never let that happen. He'd fight her for Gina, and he'd win.

Walking into her bedroom with the envelope in her hand, Linda opened her closet door and reached for the box she kept on the floor way in the back. Sitting the box on her bed, she opened it, placing today's letter among the dozens of unopened ones. Briefly tempted to read them, instead she crawled into bed and lay there thinking.

During her self-imposed isolation, Linda watched the news. She knew things weren't good. The nightly pictures were so horrifying she felt sorry for the soldiers and what they were going through. However, her anger never allowed her sympathy to extend to Donald.

As a diversion from her thoughts about Donald and the war, Linda drifted back to a happier time when she was with Joe. She imagined lying naked in their secret place high above the ocean. She remembered the feeling of his warm hands on her body and every single passionate kiss. And she heard his voice speaking words of love. She was so desperate for him it physically hurt.

Linda knew her memories were all she had, and they'd have to be enough both now and forever because she'd never love another man the way she loved Joe.

As she lay in the dark, the all too familiar voice reared its ugly head again, asking, "How will you ever care for two children? You can barely manage one." Cruelly reminding her how she'd almost killed Gina.

Linda knew she couldn't allow the old demons to take hold of her again. She knew if she did, they'd succeed this time and take everything from her.

Instead of listening to the voices in her head and feeling sorry for herself, she lay flat on her back with tears running down her face and placed her hands on either side of her belly. She whispered to her unborn baby, saying, "Little one, one day you're probably gonna hate me, but it was love that brought you to me, and I ain't sorry for it. You only say you're sorry when you've done somethin' wrong and you're ashamed of it. I ain't ever gonna be ashamed of you. I know I can't expect you to understand, but with all my heart, I pray someday you'll understand why I had to do this."

Then, doing what she'd been dreading for months, Linda wrote her one and only letter to Donald.

> *Dear Donald,*
>
> *NO, I haven't forgiven you, nor will I ever accept that leaving me and Gina here alone in Hawaii was for the best. When you left, it was my intention not to be here when you returned. As far as I was concerned, our marriage was over, but yes, I am here and yes, I've gotten all your letters. However, I haven't read one of them.*

How dare he even suggest she'd accept his actions as something in her best interest?

> *Then today, I received the one by courier, saying you're coming home.*

She paused, trying to imagine how things would be when Donald returned. It felt as if he'd been away for a lifetime. It seemed impossible to her that in such a short time she'd found true happiness, fallen in love, made a baby and survived a broken heart.

> *What I'm going to say next will be difficult for you to hear, and there isn't an easy way to say it, so I'm just going to say it.*
>
> *I'm pregnant. Who's baby it is, isn't important. What is important is the baby. I've thought of a million different ways to handle this*

situation, but the reality is, soon our family will increase and, like you said, Gina is excited about having a baby brother or sister.

That she and Donald were children who should never of gotten married and who were now trapped was no longer important. What was important was navigating this very scary adult world together.

What the future holds for us, only God knows, and I pray He will help us find our way through this situation for the children's sake. We've made lots of mistakes but that ain't these babies' fault and we owe it to them to try.

To try what? she wondered. To try living, lying? Pretending? Her loving someone else and Donald hating her for it? Linda read what she'd written over and over. It seemed cold, but it was written from a bitter heart. And while her heart might be cold, the thought of Donald not knowing he was coming home to a pregnant wife seemed much worse than receiving a cold-hearted letter.

No, no matter how much she hated Donald for making her come to Hawaii, she didn't have it in her to do that to him.

She signed it simply: *Linda.*

Kiana

She mailed the letter and waited day in and day out, now hoping for a letter from Donald. Her mind raced with question after question. What if Donald didn't get her letter? What if he came home not knowing she was pregnant? Or what if he received it and decided not to come back for her at all? The what ifs seemed endless.

The weeks passed slowly, and Linda got bigger. When she received word from Donald, all it said was he and three hundred other soldiers would arrive on January 31st. There was no mention of her letter, so she did not know if he'd received it or not.

* * *

The homecoming for Donald and the troop was nothing like their farewell. In fact, the homecoming had no fanfare. Unless, of course, you counted the thousands of protesters lining the street leading to the airport terminal. She'd seen stories on the news about the protests, but it shocked her to see it up close. As the plane landed, she watched horrified as the protestors jumped the fence and ran out on the runway carrying signs high over their heads that read; "Baby Killers," "Say no to war" and "Thou shalt not kill."

The Military Police were everywhere, with guns drawn, trying to hold the protesters at bay as they screamed things Linda would have preferred Gina not hear. She knew she should've found a sitter, but she felt stronger and braver when Gina was with her.

Excited, Gina couldn't stand still. Jumping up and down, she screamed, "Momma, do you think daddy will be happy to see us?"

"Of course, he will be happy to see us," Linda answered, deep down she wondered if Donald was even on the plane.

Some wives were standing together in groups. Linda knew what they were saying about her, but she didn't care. No matter what they said, it could never take away the best three months of her life, and she wouldn't allow them to make it dirty.

With the noise of the engine and the shouts of protestors drowning out her thoughts, Linda watched from behind dark glasses, chin up, holding onto Gina's shoulders, steadying herself.

When the door opened, they wheeled out several soldiers, and the crowds grew loud. At the sight of the wounded, some clapped, some cried, and the protestors chanted even louder.

Soldier after soldier walked down the ramp, carrying matching duffle bags, all wearing the same defeated looks on their faces. Then she saw him. His head pivoted from side to side, looking for her. Then his eyes locked on her and never looked away.

The closer Donald came, the surer Linda was that he'd received her letter. His eyes were hard and cold. The sound of Gina's squeal redirected Donald's gaze, and he dropped his duffle bag. Scooping up his daughter, he buried his face against her tiny body, holding on so tight Linda worried he was hurting her.

When he looked up, there were tears in his eyes.

Exactly why Donald was crying, Linda didn't know for sure. She knew Donald and the men like him had marched off to war proud to protect their country, and now must feel betrayed by the very ones they swore to protect. There was talk that the United States had been lied to, and Vietnam was never a threat. Donald and men like him would never believe the country they loved and fought to defend would lie to them, but Linda wasn't so sure.

Adjusting Gina in his arms, Donald picked up his duffle bag with one hand and offering her the other one. Linda hesitated; she'd seen the way he looked at her. Maybe it was for show, she didn't know, but because Linda believed this was the best thing for her children, she took his hand.

Looking up, she worried about what she might see. Would she see anger? Disappointment or, even worse, disgust? What she saw she wasn't prepared for. Donald was thinner. He looked older, and his eyes seemed even sadder than before.

Linda held her breath as she watched Donald's eyes move down her body, stopping at her belly, his eyes transfixed.

Feeling uncomfortable, Linda said, "Gina, how about we take daddy out for dinner tonight?"

Jumping up and down, Gina asked, "Can we get burgers and fries?"

"You better ask your daddy," Linda answered.

Again, the sound of his daughter's voice redirected his gaze from her protruding belly to Gina's smiling face. "You bet we can," he said.

Holding hands, the three of them walked from the tarmac toward the terminal, looking very much like a perfectly normal family.

"Daddy, guess how old I am now," Gina said. Without waiting for his answer, Gina said, "I'm past four and Momma says next year I can go to real school. I went to preschool while you were gone. Did you know that?" Then, without taking a breath, Gina added, "And guess what, I can count to fifty. Plus, I can write my name all by myself, well, sort of. I need a little help sometimes."

Before Donald could answer any of Gina's questions, she continued asking, "Are you home to stay now, Daddy? I hope so. And I'm so glad you got home before my baby sister gets here."

Laughing, Donald asked, "And what if it's a baby brother?"

"Oh, it won't be," Gina said. "I prayed and asked God for a sister and Momma says God always answers our prayers." Silently, Linda thanked God for giving her a daughter who could carry on a conversation all by herself.

Inside the terminal, the military band played a cheerful tune, and everyone seemed happy. Looking around, Linda caught sight of Jan. She knew she'd shut out her only friend and wished she'd been kinder to her.

Donald tugged lightly on her hand. "Are you ready?" he asked. She nodded, showing she was ready and, without knowing if she saw her or not, Linda waved goodbye to Jan.

As they walked out of the terminal, Linda's head and her heart screamed NO, but her body moved involuntarily, and she thought about Jan again. While some things had changed, the fact they were two lonely women trapped in loveless marriages hadn't. She wondered if one day Jan would divorce her husband and find what she was looking for. She hoped so.

As for Linda, she had her kids to think about. So, she walked out of the terminal hand in hand with Donald, once again toward an unknown future.

At home, Donald insisted on sleeping in one of the twin beds in Gina's room. Gina slept with Linda.

Neither talked about their time apart. In fact, they talked very little, both going about their days as if nothing had happened.

A few weeks later, Donald received notice they were being transferred back to Irwin Army Base. Back to where Linda longed to be until the day she met Joe. The thought of leaving Hawaii now was as terrifying as the thought of leaving California was over a year ago. Deep down, Linda knew while she was physically leaving and thousands of miles would separate them, her heart and her soul would remain in Hawaii with Joe forever.

In what seemed like a lifetime, but in reality had only been thirteen months, Linda was going home, eight months pregnant. As the plane took off, she looked out the window for one last look at what had been her home for over a year.

It hadn't been her intention to think of Joe today. She'd promised herself she wouldn't, but she was helpless to stop it. Placing her hand on the window, trying to hold back her tears, Linda silently mouthed, "Goodbye, my love, goodbye."

* * *

A month later, home and settled, Linda and Donald took right up where they'd left off. Donald played his part as the provider. She played hers as wife and mother.

Donald re-enlisted for another four years and was promoted to a higher rank. And with his promotion came a larger house with much nicer furniture, three bedrooms, and a large yard for Gina. While Donald wasn't as overly attentive as he was when she was pregnant with Gina, he wasn't cruel, either.

From their first night in the new house, although Donald had hung his clothes in her closet, he'd slept in the third bedroom. Both seemed content. Linda knew they needed to talk, but she hadn't pushed it.

Sitting across from Donald at the dinner table, Linda asked, "Can we talk?"

Looking up, Donald said, "Sure. What shall we talk about?"

"I think we need to talk about the baby," Linda said.

"Why? Obviously, I love you," Donald said.

"I didn't ask if you loved me," Linda whispered.

Setting his fork down, Donald said, "Look, I'm here for you and for Gina. Therefore, I'm here for this baby, too."

"You could've said as much," Linda said whispering.

"I'm here. Isn't that enough?" Donald asked. "I will say, though, I'm deeply hurt by your transgressions, but it's not entirely your fault. I blame myself for making you go to Hawaii, if only I…" he said, unable to finish his sentence.

"That's water under the bridge now. Isn't it?" he asked.

Agreeing, Linda said, "Yes. It's certainly too late to wonder what if?"

Donald said, "I'm disappointed you got yourself into this situation."

Linda whispered louder, "It wasn't my intention."

"Wasn't it?" Donald asked. "In your letter, you implied you were looking for a way out. Unfortunately, your way out turned out to be married."

Linda's head shot up. "You knew about Joe?" she asked.

Then Linda listened, feeling sick as Donald explained in detail how when she didn't answer his letters, he thought she was just mad at him and since she hadn't answered his letters in boot camp, he'd accepted she wasn't going to answer his letters then either.

"Then I got a letter from your mother," Donald said.

"You see, my dear, when you just disappear, people worry. Your mother wrote saying she and Mabel had both called and wrote to you. When you didn't answer, she contacted me. I kept her letter," he said. "Would you like to read it?"

Silent, and ashamed, Linda shook her head, no. She didn't need to read her momma's letter to know how concerned she must've been.

"And since I hadn't heard from you either, I hired a private investigator. He reported back, saying he was happy to report my wife was alive and seemed just fine. However, regrettably, it appeared she was having an affair with another man. Which, of course, I did not believe, but since his report included pictures, what could I say? I have those, too, if you're interested," he said, coolly.

Again, Linda shook her head, no.

"So, I wrote her back assuring her you were fine, and were having an affair," Donald said bluntly.

Knowing Donald told her momma about her affair, Linda's anger flared, and she was no longer silent. "How dare you? You had no right tellin' my momma anything. What I do ain't nobody's business but mine," Linda yelled.

"I had no right?" Donald yelled back. "Do you really think my wife having sex with another man is none of my business?"

Knowing Gina could hear them, Linda whispered, "Please, let's not yell."

Then, lowering his voice to barely a whisper, Donald said, "It was difficult enough knowing you were having an affair, but when I received your letter saying you were pregnant, it devastated me, but I still love you. So, your baby will have my name and as soon as he or she is born, we'll resume our married life."

Resume their married life! Linda knew exactly what Donald meant. He meant they'd be resuming their sex life. After the love she'd shared with Joe, having sex with Donald again seemed unimaginable.

Still whispering, Donald asked, "This is what you wanted, right? For me to accept your love child as mine. For us all to be one big happy family."

The voice inside her head screamed, HELL, NO! That's not what I want! This time, Linda nodded her head yes. Not for her sake, but for her girls.

Then Donald stood up with such force his chair fell over. Taking Linda by the arms none too gently, he lifted her out of the chair and said, "Then it's settled." He let go of her arm and walked out of the room.

* * *

Linda slept peacefully, dreaming she was back in Hawaii. She saw herself, completely naked, standing high on a cliff. Joe was with her, and he was smiling. He was about to take her in his arms and lay her down on the green grass when a pain shot through her belly. Her eyes flew open, and she lay perfectly still, trying to determine if the pain was real or part of the dream. Then the pain came again, and her water broke, soaking the bed.

Linda panted through the contraction and when it passed she got up, stripped the bed, and got dressed. Remembering the night before, she wished she could just get in the car and drive herself to the hospital. Swallowing her pride, she picked up her bag, and walked down the hall to wake up Donald.

A few hours later, Linda brought her second child into the world, a six-pound baby girl. Tears of joy ran down her cheeks as the nurse handed her a tightly wrapped bundle. She could feel her tiny heartbeat through the blanket. Drying her tears, Linda pulled the blanket back, looking at her daughter for the first time. This baby had Linda's hair color, but nothing else. Her skin was dark and though her eyes were closed, she knew without a doubt they were the same shape and color as Joe's.

Before Linda was ready, the nurse returned, taking her baby saying, "We need to get you moved to the ward. I promise I'll bring her back to you soon. Does she have a name yet?" the nurse asked.

"Yes. Her name is Kiana Linn," Linda answered.

* * *

Linda spent the two days in the hospital alone, getting acquainted with her daughter. When Kiana was hungry, she fed her. When she was wet, she changed her and when she was sleepy, Linda rocked her gently, singing softly to her. And in between times, Linda talked candidly to Kiana, telling her all about her father. Sharing every intimate detail, she said, "Kiana, I want you to know I love your father with all my heart, and I always will. And since I can't give him my love, I'm gonna give it all to you. I promise I'm gonna love you and care for you the best I know how. You should know though, I ain't done a great job with your sister, but I'm gonna try to do better with you," Linda promised.

Knowing she'd be going home soon and cherished every moment alone with Kiana, her peace and joy was lost when the nurse came in to announce she and Kiana had a visitor.

Panic struck, and Linda's heart raced. She hadn't seen Donald since the day Kiana was born, and she wasn't ready to see him yet.

"Please," Linda said, "I'm tired and Kiana is sleeping. Could you tell him I can't have visitors right now?"

"Oh, I think you'll like this visitor," the nurse said, smiling and taking Kiana from her arms.

Confused, Linda asked, "Who is it?"

"It's this little girl's big sister," the nurse said, "and she's eager to meet her. However, children aren't allowed on the maternity ward, so your husband and daughter are down on the lawn under your window. Let's get you up. Then you can hold Kiana up to the window for them to see."

She put on her robe and slippers and took Kiana in her arms. Pulling the curtain back, she saw Gina jumping up and down with excitement and waved at her. Pushing the blanket back from Kiana's face, she held her up so Gina could see her. Then she waved again, blew a kiss to Gina, and dropped the curtain, never once looking at Donald.

* * *

On the third day of Kiana's life, Donald pushed Linda down the long hall in a wheelchair. Kiana slept in her arms and Gina walked beside them. To all who noticed, they looked like the picture-perfect family.

In the car, Gina asked, "Momma, when we get home, can I hold my sister?"

"Yes, if she's not sleeping," she answered.

"I want to play with her," Gina whined.

Smiling at Gina, Linda said, "One day your baby sister will be big enough to play with, but it's gonna be a while. And besides, you'll be starting school soon, then you'll make lots of friends and you won't have time to play with your sister."

"Gina, how about we take Momma and Kiana home, and you and I go get hamburgers for dinner," Donald suggested to Gina.

Excited, Gina started jumping up and down in the backseat. "Oh, and milkshakes, too?" Gina asked, in a high-pitched scream.

Linda frowned slightly at Donald as Kiana started crying.

"Yes, we can, but I need you to do something for me first," Donald whispered.

Confused, Gina asked, "What?"

"I need you to talk quieter because your sister is sleeping," Donald said.

Putting her hand over mouth. Gina said, "Oops, I'm sorry, Daddy."

Linda laughed, knowing this was just one of a thousand times they were going to have to remind Gina to keep her voice down.

Donald's Confession

The first month of Kiana's life was blissful for Linda. Then on the day she turned six weeks old, everything changed.

Linda and Gina were watching cartoons and Kiana was asleep in her bassinet when Donald came home unexpectedly.

"Are you okay?" Linda whispered.

Shutting off the TV, Donald answered, "I'm fine."

Tears welled up in Gina's eyes when Donald said, "Gina, you need to go into your room and play."

"No, Daddy," Gina said. "I don't want to go to my room. I'm watching The Roadrunner."

Donald's voice got louder yelling, "Gina Marie, I said go to your room. now!"

"Gina, do as your daddy said and be quiet. Your sister's sleeping," Linda said.

Bursting into tears, Gina yelled at the top of her lungs, "Why do I always have to be quiet?" Then she ran into her room, slamming the door, causing Kiana to jump.

As soon as she was sure Gina couldn't hear them, Linda asked, "What the hell is wrong with you? Are you sick or somethin'?"

"No, I'm fine. I'm just tired," Donald answered, sitting down.

"Why? Aren't you sleeping well?" Linda asked.

"No, I'm not," he answered. "And because I'm not sleeping well is why I've decided tonight I'll be sleeping in my own bed."

Feeling like someone had punched her in the stomach, Linda said, "I'm perfectly happy with things the way they are."

"Yes, you seem quite content, but I am not," Donald said.

Although she already knew the answer, she asked anyway, "What is it you want?"

"I came home to a pregnant wife. Do you even have to ask that question?" he yelled? When Linda did not respond, Donald continued, "I've been patient, Linda."

"Okay fine. Kiana and I will move into your room," Linda said.

"You can move Kiana's bassinet in there if you'd like, but you'll be sleeping with me!" Donald yelled.

"Donald, Kiana is only six weeks old. She's up and down all night. You still won't get any sleep. Please, things are fine the way they are. Maybe when she's a little older," Linda said, hoping he'd see she wasn't saying never, just not now.

"Yes, things have been fine for you," Donald said. "Like I said, Linda, I've been patient. You have everything. You have your baby, and she has my name, and I think you owe me a little gratitude."

"Gratitude for what, Donald?" Linda asked. "Gratitude for forcing me to go to Hawaii? You left me there alone. No family, no friends, scared out of my mind, and you expect me to thank you for it?"

"Scared?" Donald yelled. "Were you scared when you went bar hopping? Were you scared when you spread your legs for another man? And now, because you were scared, I'm expected to raise another man's baby without the benefit of a wife. No, now you will spread your legs for your husband."

Without thinking, Linda slapped Donald so hard her hand hurt, but the pain was nothing compared to the pain she felt when Donald's fist connected with her jaw. Linda hit the floor just as Gina ran out of her room and Kiana started crying.

The remorse on Donald's face was apparent as he tried to help her up, begging for forgiveness. Linda pushed his hand away, then, taking Gina by the hand, she walked into her bedroom, locking the door behind her.

"Momma, why did daddy hit you?" Gina asked.

"Everything's fine Gina, your daddy was just mad," Linda answered.

"Is daddy gonna hit me when he's mad, Momma?" Gina asked.

"No, your daddy wouldn't hit you, ever," Linda assured Gina.

"Momma, I'm scared. Can I stay here with you and Kiana?" she asked.

"Yes, sweetie," Linda said, "climb up in here and I'll read you a story."

"I don't have a book Momma, they're all in my room," Gina said.

"It's okay sweetie," she said, climbing into bed, "we'll sing instead."

A short time later, Linda heard Donald at the door, and she held her breath, wondering what he might do when he found the door locked. Then the sound of the front door closing and Donald driving away was music to Linda's ears. She got up quietly, opened the bedroom door cautiously, making sure she truly was alone. She locked the front door, sat down at the table and called home. Crying, she told her momma about Joe and about Kiana.

The next morning, Linda got up early, packed some clothes and called a cab, praying it'd get there before Donald did.

"Where are we going, Momma?" Gina asked.

"We going to go visit your grandma Irma," Linda answered.

"Grandma Irma? Do I know her? Where does she live?" Gina asked.

Linda was trying to answer Gina's questions when she heard Donald's car pull into the driveway.

Donald was quick to notice the suitcase sitting at the front door and asked, "Where do you think you're going?"

"I'm going to visit momma and daddy," Linda answered.

Turning to Gina, Donald shouted, "Gina, go to your room!" Scared and crying, Gina ran to her room, slamming the door.

"Linda, what happened last night will never happen again, I promise. Please unpack your things," Donald pleaded.

Looking up at Donald, Linda said, "No Donald, I ain't unpackin'."

Linda could see the rage in his eyes. His face turned red as he turned away from her and walked toward Kiana, who was asleep in her baby carrier. No longer scared for herself, now scared for her baby, Linda ran toward Kiana, but Donald beat her to the carrier. Picking it up by the handle, he held it above his head, demanding Linda have sex with him now or he would drop her.

Terrified, Linda stared, watching like a spectator at the movies as Donald stood poised with Kiana above his head.

Gina ran out of her room screaming, "Daddy, put my sister down!" Donald didn't move. His eyes spoke volumes, daring her to refuse him.

Linda stared back. Again Donald didn't budge. Not knowing what else to do, she whispered, "Okay Donald, you win. Just give me the baby."

Then the look in his eyes changed, as if to say he didn't believe her.

"Donald," Linda said as calmly as she could, "I promise I will have sex with you. Right now if you'd like. I'll just put Kiana in her crib and I will meet you in the bedroom."

While Linda pleaded, Gina screamed repeatedly. "Daddy put my sister down," pounding on his leg.

The sound of Gina's crying voice brought Donald back to his senses, and he set the carrier down at Linda's feet. There were tears in his eyes as he turned and walked into the bedroom, slamming the door behind him.

* * *

Day by day, Linda went through the motions. At night, when Donald touched her, unable to get the picture of Donald threatening to drop Kiana out of her head, Linda pulled away. For her, the damage was done, and she couldn't pretend everything was okay. This only caused more ugly fights and a lot of sleepless nights for them both. Gina became more difficult and started disappearing. Sometimes she just hid from Linda. Other times she'd take off and Linda had to hunt her down in the neighborhood. Secretly, Linda could not wait for the day Gina would start school.

* * *

Kiana was in her crib, wet and crying, as Linda ran from room to room looking frantically for Gina when the phone rang. Mainly just to stop the noise, Linda answered, screaming "Hello!" over Kiana's crying.

It was her momma for the third time in a week. "Hey Momma," Linda said, "the baby's crying and I can't find Gina. I gotta call you back later," hanging up the phone.

Running to the crib, she picked up Kiana and ran to the back door, quickly scanning the yard, hoping Gina was there, but she wasn't.

Back in the house, she lay Kiana down again, and ran as fast as she could to the front door, praying Gina was in the front yard and safe.

Instead of finding her playing quietly in the yard, she found a man standing in the doorway holding Gina in his arms, her foot wrapped in a towel and the towel soaked in blood.

"Oh, my God, what happen? Gina, I was frantic. Where were you?" Linda asked, nearly breaking down crying.

Tearfully Gina answered, "I was crossing the street to play with Missy and there was glass in the road and I stepped on it."

"I was driving past and saw her sitting out on the curb crying," the man said. "Hi, my name is Pete."

Ignoring him, Linda scolded Gina, saying, "Gina Marie, you know you ain't supposed to cross the street by yourself."

"I'm sorry Momma," Gina said.

Turning to the stranger in her living room, Linda said, "I'm sorry I didn't get your name."

"My name is Pete. I live a few blocks over. I was on my way home," the stranger answered.

"Pete, thank you for bringing her home," Linda said. Hoping he'd let himself out, Linda turned her attention to Gina's foot. The cut was deep. Sure it needed stitching, she called Donald.

When Donald answered, all Linda could say was, "Gina's cut her foot and needs to go to the emergency room," and she hung up.

Crying, Gina said, "Momma, I'm sorry."

"I know sweetie, let's talk about it later." Kiana started crying again and in frustration, Linda looked up at the ceiling, praying out loud, "Dear God, I'm about to lose my mind here. Please help." Fifteen minutes later, Donald rushed in and after taking a quick look at Gina's foot, he agreed she needed to go to the hospital.

Finally able to tend to Kiana, Linda changed her, fed her, and sang her to sleep. Then she sat down, lit a cigarette, hung her head, and cried uncontrollably, feeling like an utter failure.

"Dear God," she cried. How could things have gone so very wrong? Was it Hawaii? Vietnam? Or were we doomed from the beginning?

* * *

When Donald returned from the ER, he sat Gina on the couch and said, "Well, it only took three stitches. However, because the stitches are at the bottom of her foot, the doctor says she needs to stay off it until the stitches come out. Otherwise, they may not hold. If the stitches don't hold and the doctor has to restitch her, she'll be in a cast until her foot heals."

"And how long before the stitches come out?" Linda asked.

"Ten days," Donald answered as he turned and walked away.

Tired and cried out, Gina fell asleep at one end of the couch watching cartoons. Kiana was awake playing in her crib, so Linda laid down on the other end and watched Gina sleep.

She'd just begun enjoying the peace and quiet when the phone rang again. Sure it was her momma again, but worried the ringing would wake Gina, Linda ran to the phone and answered it.

"Hello," Linda whispered. Devoid of emotion, she listened as Donald yelled. He said she was favoring Joe's baby and neglecting his and called her an unfit mother. When the string of hurtful words turned to her neglect of him in the bedroom, she hung up.

Leaving the front door open so she could hear Gina if she woke up, Linda stepped out onto the front porch and lit a cigarette. Within seconds, the phone rang again. This time, she ignored it.

With the weight of the world sitting on her shoulders, Linda walked back into the house and sat down on the couch next to Gina and whispered in her ear, "I don't know how I am supposed to keep you down, Gina Marie. I know this though: if you wanna to go to kindergarten like a big girl, then you better start bein' a good girl."

Across the hall, Kiana was in her crib, playing with her toes. Fighting back threatening tears, Linda scooped up Kiana, squeezing her tight until Kiana fussed.

"Oh sweetie, I'm sorry, I just love you so much," she said, laying her back down.

Hearing the front door open, then close quietly, Linda looked up to find Donald standing in the doorway; he looked sad.

Wondering which of Donald's personalities she'd encounter this time, she prayed it was the silent one because she was too tired to fight.

Picking up Kiana, she walked straight toward Donald, hoping he'd let her pass. He did.

Linda was balancing Kiana on her hip, warming her bottle, when Donald walked into the kitchen. Expecting more of his vicious words, it surprised her when Donald held out his arms, saying, "Here, let me help."

Linda wasn't sure exactly what he was up to, but she allowed it.

Cooing in his best baby voice, Donald said, "Come to daddy."

With the warm bottle in hand, Linda reached out to take Kiana back, but Donald asked, "Can I feed her?" Again, she noted his sad look.

Saying nothing, Linda handed Donald the bottle.

"It's been a few years," he said, laughing. "I think I remember how, though."

Coolly Linda said, "Okay, if you're sure, then I'll go check on Gina. She's been sound asleep ever since you brought her home."

When Linda walked back into the kitchen, Kiana was almost asleep, so she tiptoed to the sink and lit a cigarette.

"See, I remember how to feed a baby," Donald said.

"Yes, I see." Curious, Linda asked, "Why the sudden interest in feeding my baby?"

Donald's smile faded, and he hung his head as if ashamed. Then, without answering Linda's question, Donald said, "I was wrong to say the things I said on the phone. Please forgive me. I know I've said and done things lately that are inexcusable and I'm so sorry," Donald said.

In the months since his return, Linda encountered the many sides of Donald. There were times he was silent and sad. Other times angry and downright mean, but never remorseful.

Continuing, Donald said, "I know I don't deserve your forgiveness, but I'm asking for it. Can you find it in your heart to forgive me?"

Confused and proceeding cautiously, Linda walked over and took Kiana out of his arms.

Donald let Kiana go, saying, "Please come back. We need to talk."

Linda took her time changing Kiana's diaper. Then she pulled the blanket up over her, patting her lightly on the back, and hummed a little tune until she fell back asleep.

With both girls asleep, Linda wanted to go to bed. The day had been long and stressful, but she couldn't get Donald's question out of her mind. Could she forgive him for the last few months? Could she forgive his words? His actions? Did she even want to forgive him? Maybe there were just too many things to be forgiven.

Linda sat down at the table with these questions swirling around and around in her head, lit two cigarettes, handed one to Donald, and waited.

Looking down at his lap, speaking in a low tone, Donald said, "When our ship left Hawaii in route for in Vũng Tàu, South Vietnam, I couldn't believe the number of tanks, guns, ammo and even missiles that were onboard. And ours was just one of many ships the US sent. Every night I prayed we were not bombed because we were one huge floating explosion waiting to happen. When our ship docked safely, I was sure we would not be there long. I figured the Viet Cong would surrender quickly to our military forces because they seemed so massive."

He stopped long enough to take a drag of his cigarette, then continued, saying, "The night we arrived, there was no moon and very few stars in the sky. I didn't know what time it was, but it had to be after midnight and was 100 degrees outside and humid. Then it began raining, and I remember being grateful for the rain. I thought it would cool us off," he said, laughing.

"It took hours, but eventually we got off the ship and loaded on to land transports by our regiment number. We traveled slowly for hours, bouncing up and down and side to side, sweaty, on terrible roads, in the pitch black. When we stopped, a regiment number would be called. Random like, you know?" he said, looking up. "So, you never knew when they'd call your number. We'd been told when our number was called to be prepared to jump up and off because the transports didn't linger. My regiment number was one of the last ones to be called."

Linda listened for the next two hours, mesmerized, while Donald talked of places he'd been, the things he'd seen and done. Things she couldn't even imagine. When he finally looked up, there were tears in his eyes saying, "There's more you need to know."

'I'm sure there is," Linda said, "but I'm gettin' hungry. Why don't you check on the girls while I make dinner?"

They ate in silence, then Linda cleaned the kitchen, made a bottle for Kiana, and waited for Donald to speak again.

Linda was about to suggest they go to bed and finish the conversation in the morning when Donald proceeded with his story, saying, "In Vietnam, every day I woke up wondered if waking up was a blessing or a curse. We traveled by day on foot and when we could set up camp, our job was to protect the Vietnamese from the Viet Cong in the area. However, we never stayed very long in one place.

"On the days I wasn't on duty, I liked to walk up the rice patty lined roads alone, and I always took my gun," he said, lighting a cigarette.

"There were days so hot there, you'd be so wet from your own sweat your clothes stuck to you. And just when you thought you couldn't get any wetter, the sky opened up and it would rain. And when it rained, you just got hotter and wetter. After the rain, the mud puddles made it hard to walk. Oh, but it was beautiful," he said, sighing.

"Then one day I was out walking, and I stumbled on a Vietnamese family hiding in the reeds along the road. They hid their heads in fear at first, then realizing I was an American, they were happy to see me. The Vietnamese knew that when a soldier was present, he was armed, and they were safer. I waved them out of the reeds, letting them know it was okay and since I didn't have anywhere to be, I followed them at a distance. We hadn't gone far when they stopped, waiting for me to catch up."

Donald took a drag of his cigarette, then continued, "The oldest of the group of eight pointed to a small encampment, then signaled me to follow him. Curious, I followed them. The man stopped in front of a makeshift house—the walls were made with bamboo shoots tied together with long strands of grass. Scraps of wood laid on the ground resembled a porch and there was no door, just a curtain made from rice sacks covered the opening. The elder pointed at me, then to the hut. Inside, he pointed again toward the table, which contained bowls of food. I tried to say no, but he insisted, pushing me into a rough wooden chair. It was no use arguing. They didn't speak English, and I didn't speak Vietnamese. Not wanting to offend them, I ate."

"As we sat around the table, they talked and laughed among themselves. And although I didn't know what they were saying, soon I was laughing right along with them. When we finished eating, I pulled a pack of cigarettes out of my pocket and passed it around—my contribution to the meal. As the hours passed, I knew I should leave, but I couldn't. It was as if I'd found a family, strange as it was, a much-needed family," he said. Pausing, he looked up and said, "See, you weren't the only lonely one."

Exhausted, longing for bed, but riveted by every word, Linda wondered where he was going with the story. Then he said, "There was a young girl there, sitting at the far end of the table, and every time our eyes met, she smiled at me. Being a lonely man, far away from home, I knew exactly what my male needs were, so I did my best not to make eye contact with her, as I imagined her wrapped in my arms, naked and willing. I knew my thoughts were wrong, but I couldn't help myself. Do you know what I mean?" Donald asked.

Linda knew exactly what Donald meant. She remembered her own loneliness and fears all too well. "Yes," she answered, feeling she now knew where this was going. "Please go on," she said, noticing the deeper Donald got into his story, the happier his face looked, and the more he relaxed.

Continuing, Donald said, "I left the encampment happy, fulfilled somehow. It seemed silly, being happy after a day of eating strange food with strangers and laughing with them. For all I knew, they were laughing at me. Still, I laughed right along with them. It felt so good to laugh and for a few hours, I forgot all about my own fears because I was protecting them. So, I started going to see them whenever I could. I showed up with cigarettes to smoke and they shared their food."

Then Donald stopped. Looking up, he said, "I'm sorry, I should let you go to bed." Afraid if they stopped now, she may never hear the rest of the story, Linda said, "No, please go on, I'm listening."

Smiling, Donald said, "Each time I visited, they greeted me with big smiles and led me to the table, where we'd eat, laugh, and smoke for hours."

His voice turned serious, and he said, "And each time I visited, the young girl sat closer and closer until eventually she was sitting beside me. There was one adult man for every adult woman who lived in their hovel, and I noticed each woman served one man and her own kids. Except for Lily, that's what I named her. She served herself. Then one day Lily served me, which seemed to make all of them happy."

Clearing his throat, Donald continued, "At first, I was confused, then it became clear they were offering Lily to me in exchange for protection. I had very little to offer them in the way of protection because I knew any day my regiment could move up the line and I'd be gone."

"After that," Donald said, "I stayed away for a while, wrestling with my feelings, hoping we'd pull up stakes. Until finally, lonely for my newfound family, I returned and accepted their gift."

Linda wanted to be mad, but she wasn't. How could she be, remembering her own loneliness and how she'd been helpless to stop her own affair. She knew Donald had been, too. They were both victims of war.

"Can you forgive me?" Donald asked again.

"Donald, please don't ask me that," Linda whispered. She knew if she forgave him, she'd have to ask him for forgiveness, too.

In Linda's mind, you only ask for forgiveness when you've done something wrong. So, by asking for forgiveness, she'd be admitting she'd done something wrong, making Kiana a mistake. No, she couldn't forgive or be forgiven. She just wanted to forget and start over.

* * *

She sat with her head down, tears silently rolled down her face. Her heart pounded and her mind reeled as Donald walked over and pulled her up and out of her chair. Crushing her against him, he kissed her long and hard. She was helpless to stop him, and she didn't want to. They kissed with such passion it caused her head to hurt. She knew if they were going to save their marriage, they'd have to come to terms with their betrayals. And she knew one day they would. However, the pure, raw emotion of his kisses was driving her to crazy heights, and Linda longed to be naked in Donald's arms.

"Oh, my Linda, I need you now. Right here," Donald moaned.

"Shh! Gina's in the living room," she whispered as he moaned again.

"It's ok. I've got an idea. Wait for me in the backyard," she whispered.

After making sure both girls were asleep, Linda rummaged through her dresser drawer until she found the silk night gown her momma had given her as a wedding present. Determined not to think about the things that had happened leading up to this moment, Linda undressed and slipped the nightgown down over her naked body. She put on her robe, grabbed the comforter off their bed, and walked out the back door to her waiting husband.

As she spread the blanket on the ground she felt Donald's arms wrap around her.

He whispered, "What took so long? I missed you."

Letting her robe fall to the ground, Linda said, "It took me a while to find this old thing."

Resuming Married Life

It was a sunny Sunday morning. Linda was lying in bed, truly happy, reflecting on the last few months. Gina's foot healed up, and she started school right on time. Kiana was walking and was everywhere at once. And she and Donald seemed to have found their way back to each other, something she still couldn't believe. Donald told her daily he loved her, but Linda didn't care if he did or not. They'd found common ground, and that was good enough for her.

It was like a miracle took place the night Donald confessed his infidelities to her. He'd gone from cold and withdrawn to being a good father. He was attentive to her and took part in helping with both girls. And finally, Linda was the wife and mother even she could be proud of.

On weekend mornings, Donald would get the girls up and let her sleep in. Linda had slept better in the last few months than in her twenty-five years on the earth. She was saying a quick prayer, thanking God for all her blessings, when she heard the phone ring.

As she entered the kitchen, Donald, holding his hand over the receiver, said, "It's your mother. What shall I tell her?" Donald asked. "She says it's important."

Reaching for the phone, she said, "I'll take it. She's just gonna keep callin' if I don't."

Smiling, Donald handed her the phone asking, "Shall I warm up your breakfast now?"

Smiling sweetly, Linda said, "Please, hopefully this won't take too long," dragging the long cord into the living room.

This was the one thing that was not so good in Linda's world. Her momma and her daddy were on and off again. Their drinking was out of control. Her brother Arnie moved out and was living with the church's pastor and his family. Unfortunately, there wasn't anything she could do but listen, so she did.

A half hour later, Linda walked into the kitchen and, seeing her plate on the table, said, "Oh Donald, I'm so sorry."

"It's fine. Is everything okay?" he asked.

"No, not really. Momma says daddy moved out again and this time she doesn't think he comin' back."

"What do you think?" Donald asked.

"I think my parents are heading for a divorce," Linda answered.

"And what will your momma do if he doesn't come back?" Donald asked.

"I've got no idea, but I promise you, it won't be movin' in here. Maybe she can live with Mabel," she said.

Kissing her on the cheek, Donald said, "Okay, I'm off to the range. I'll be back before dinner."

After Donald left, humming, Linda cleaned up the breakfast dishes and just sat down, intending to work on dinner plans for Donald's birthday the following week, when the phone rang.

Linda took a deep breath and answered the phone, "Hello again, Momma."

"Mrs. Holloway, this is Captain Johns, at the range. I'm sorry to tell you this, ma'am, Private First-Class Holloway had an accident. He's been taken by ambulance to the hospital emergency room, here on the base. Do you know where it is?" he asked.

"Yes, I know where the emergency room is, but can you tell me what happened?" she asked as she sat down.

"All I know is he fell off his rig and took a blow to the head," he said.

With tears in her eyes, Linda said, "I can't get to the hospital. Donald took our car and I've got no way to get there. And I'm alone here with my kids. Is he gonna to be all right?" she asked.

"I don't know ma'am, he was unconscious when he left here," he said.

Feeling sick to her stomach, Linda said, "Okay, I'll call the hospital right away." Linda said a quick prayer asking God to look after Donald and give her the strength to manage whatever was coming. What if Donald died from his injuries? They'd gotten so close over the last few months. The thought of losing him now seemed unbearable.

* * *

Donald's fall required several stitches and earned him a week's stay in the hospital with a very serious concussion. He'd been home from the hospital for two weeks, experiencing excruciating headaches he was unable to return to work. His temper ran from bad to worse most days.

Linda did her best to understand how frustrating it must be, still his taking it out on her and the girls was getting harder to deal with each day.

She was in the kitchen making Gina's lunch the day she'd finally had enough of his constant whining and complaining. This time, he was upset because Kiana was standing in front of the television. He couldn't see, so he yelled at Linda to come and move her.

"I'm makin' Gina's lunch," Linda yelled back. "Please, just get up and move her."

"I don't want to get up and move her!" Donald yelled. "She's your baby. You get in here and move her."

Furious, Linda flew out of the kitchen wielding a butter knife like a dangerous weapon. "Listen here, you son of a bitch," was what she wished she could say, but Gina was in the room. So calmly, Linda said, "Gina, please go play in your room for a bit."

Making sure Gina was in her room with the door shut, Linda turned, asking, "So, are we back to that? Now, Kiana is my baby?"

"You know what I meant," Donald said, trying to look around her at the television.

"Yes, I know what you meant. You meant exactly what you said. You think of Kiana as my baby?" Regretting the words as they came out of her mouth, Linda said, "How about I just take my girls and leave?"

"And just how are you going to support yourself?" Donald asked.

"I can get a job," Linda said.

Donald asked, "And who the hell is going to hire you?"

"What makes you think I can't get a job?" Linda asked.

"Because you have no education, for one," Donald answered.

"That ain't true. I got an education. I just ain't got a diploma to prove it," Linda said.

"And sadly, no one will hire you without it," he reminded her.

Linda was speechless. Donald was right. And what made it worse, she couldn't even point out the fact he didn't have one either. He was a man, and for men, it was different. Without a diploma, all Linda was qualified to be was a wife and mother, and some days, even that was questionable.

Donald got up and moved Kiana from in front of the television, turned up the volume, and sat back down.

Furious, Linda grabbed her wallet and car keys and walked out the door, yelling over her shoulder, "I'm goin' to the commissary, keep an eye on my girls."

She drove the long way around to the store, taking her time, noticing nothing along the way. As she pulled into the parking stall, tears came to her eyes, which she fought back, thinking, *No! No more tears.* She was done with crying. She wasn't sure just how much more of their fighting she could take, though.

Frustrated and in pain, Donald would say something mean or complain about something stupid. In retaliation, Linda would say something back and they'd fight. She'd considered calling his doctor, but, worried she'd upset him, Linda did nothing.

She was sitting in the car feeling sorry for herself, when she heard a knock on her car window. Looking up, she saw a face from the past. It was Diane, the wife of Donald's friend David.

Rolling down the window, Linda said, "Hello. How are you?"

"We're fine," Diane answered and asked, "When did you guys get back?"

"I've been meanin' to call you, but the girls keep me so busy and with Donald's accident, well, you know," Linda said.

"Did you say, girls? And what accident?" Diane asked.

Realizing she'd said girls, Linda said, "Yes, a one-year-old baby girl. Her name is Kiana Linn."

"A one-year-old?" Diane asked. "Was she born in Hawaii? And what about Donald's accident? Did that happen while he was in Vietnam?"

Nervous and talking way too fast, Linda said, "No, Kiana was born here, and Donald's accident was here, on the base, a month ago."

Diane said, "So, you've been back for over a year and haven't called us?"

"I know and I'm sorry Diane, but we'll have to discuss this another time. How about we get together when Donald goes back to work? I will tell you everything then," Linda said. She pulled out of the parking lot and drove straight home.

Parked safely at home in her driveway, she sat in the car shaking. This was going to happen eventually and Linda knew it was time for them to face the facts. They could not hide from the world forever.

Except for Donald's accident, the last few months had been so wonderful that until today she'd almost forgotten about Hawaii. Thoughts of Joe crept in from time to time. Linda purposely pushed them away, trying to convince herself she was happy, hiding from the inevitable.

When Linda walked into the kitchen, Donald was on the phone saying, "Yes, Ma, I know, and I promise we'll visit just as soon as we can." Linda listened to Donald making excuses for why they hadn't come to visit them yet, apologizing repeatedly. When he finally got off the phone, he put his head in his hands, rocking back and forth, obviously suffering from another headache.

Unsure but determined, Linda said, "Please Donald, we need to talk."

"Not now Linda," Donald yelled.

Ignoring him, Linda said, "I ran into Diane at the commissary, and she asked why we hadn't called them. Now I get home and your momma's callin' wonderin' why we ain't come to see them."

She paused, allowing time for Donald to speak. When he didn't, Linda went on.

"We've lived in a bubble for the last year," she said. "It wasn't easy for me to tell my momma and daddy about Kiana. Donald, this ain't your doin'. It's mine, and I am ready to let the chips fall where there gonna fall and for our families to meet Kiana."

Donald hadn't moved. He sat with his head down and his eyes closed. He stopped rocking and appeared to be listening, so she went on.

"Things were good before your accident, and they will be good again. It's just gonna take a little more time," Linda said.

The explosion that followed was terrifying. Linda sat frozen while Donald screamed in her face. He ranted about everything and nothing at the same time. One minute he screamed unpleasant things she hoped he didn't mean. The next he was talking to someone else far away. Linda watched, fascinated, when Donald's face softened, and he looked happy. Apparently talking to himself, then he said the name Lily and Linda made the connection: he was talking to his Vietnamese lover.

The look on his face changed with each conversation. He went from angry to sorry. Then from sorry to gentle and even to loving.

Linda said nothing while he talked. She hadn't forgotten the feel of his fist upon her jaw, and he didn't seem like himself right now.

When it appeared Donald was winding down, Linda asked gently, "Are you finished?"

Donald didn't answer, which didn't surprise her. Leaving him at the kitchen table, Linda went to check on her girls.

"Momma, is daddy gonna to be okay?" Gina asked.

Hoping she wasn't lying, Linda said, "Yes baby, your daddy'll be fine."

* * *

Although there were no more outbursts or fights, Donald retreated into silent mode again. Linda mentioned nothing else about going to see their families or calling David and Diane and, a month later, Donald went back to work.

Although it was obvious to Linda Donald was in denial, she was not. They couldn't hide away forever, and she knew it. They had another beautiful daughter now, and it's about time people met her.

So, determined to move on, if not with Donald, then by herself, Linda picked up the phone and dialed Diane's number, suggesting they meet for lunch the following afternoon at the Roadside Cafe.

Linda found a table at the back of the café, ordered a soda, and waited. She'd finished her soda, smoked two cigarettes and was about to leave when Diane finally showed up looking as if she'd been crying.

Worried, Linda asked, "Is everything okay?"

Looking devastated, Diane said, "David asked me for a divorce."

Reaching across the table, she took Diane's hand, saying, "I'm so sorry." Then she sat for the next hour and listened sympathetically as Diane poured out the details of her derailed marriage. Looking at her watch, Linda finally said, "I am sorry, Diane. I've gotta go pick up Gina from school now."

Picking up her purse and the check, she turned to say goodbye when Diane said, "Wait, we didn't talk about you and Donald. I want to know everything. How was Hawaii? And a baby? How did that happen?" she asked. "Please, can't you stay a little while longer?"

Taking a deep breath and exhaling slowly, Linda said, "It's a long story and right now, I don't got time to tell it. The condensed version is this: Hawaii was beautiful. It's where I fell madly in love with a man named Joe and where I got pregnant with my daughter, Kiana.

Linda watched the shock as it registered on Diane's face.

"I'm sorry. I didn't mean to pry," Diane said, apologetically.

"No need to be sorry. I don't regret a minute of it. Don't get me wrong, I am sorry I hurt Donald, but Hawaii was the highlight of my life," Linda said.

Suddenly not caring if she was late picking up the girls, Linda lit a cigarette, explaining, "When Donald left, I was scared, alone, and mad at the world. Then I met Joe, and it was like breathing air for the first time." Linda's face lit up just remembering it. "It was like, suddenly my life had meaning. When I was with Joe, I felt alive, and I wanted to live. I loved him, and he loved me, too."

"Why aren't you with Joe in Hawaii, then?" Diane asked.

"Because Joe has a wife and six kids."

"Oh, I'm sorry. That must've hurt finding out," Diane said.

Again, Linda said "Don't be sorry. I knew he was married all along."

"Wow. How is Donald with all of this? He must be angry."

"Yes," Linda answered, "I suppose he is."

Drawn back to the clock, Linda said, "Listen, I really gotta go. I'll call you soon."

Back in the car, Linda knew she'd probably made a mistake telling Diane about Hawaii and Kiana, but it was a bit too late to worry about it now.

When Linda got home, the phone was ringing. It was Donald. Yelling, he said, "How dare you go behind my back and tell Diane about your affair and about the baby? Don't you ever think about anyone else besides yourself? What about me?" Donald yelled, "Didn't you think about me?"

"You're right Donald," Linda said calmly. "I was only thinkin' of myself, and do you wanna know why? I'll tell you why. Because it was my indiscretion. It's my story to tell." Then, not caring if Gina heard her or not, Linda said, "But don't worry Donald, I didn't tell her about your little indiscretion with Lily."

The more she talked, the madder she got, "Tell me Donald, what do you got to be ashamed of? In this story, you come out lookin' like the hero and me the harlot!" When Donald didn't respond, Linda hung up the phone, without saying goodbye.

* * *

Dinner was on the dining room table when Donald got home, but he refused to eat. The sound of the bedroom door slamming caused Gina to jump and Kiana to cry.

She bathed both girls and put them to bed and was on her way to the garage with an arm full of laundry when the phone rang. It was her momma, drunk and crying.

The emotions of the day had taken everything she had and feeling like she was losing her mind, Linda yelled into the phone, "For God's sake Momma, you and Daddy need to just get a damn divorce. For everyone's sake, you gotta stop playing these games. It ain't right."

Immediately sorry and feeling like a hypocrite, Linda said, "I'm sorry, Momma. Who am I to tell you how to live your life? Hell, I can't even figure out what's goin' on in my own." Then yawning, she said, "It's been a long day. Good night, Momma," and hung up the phone.

The next day Diane called to apologize, but Linda assured her there was nothing to be sorry for. She knew it was for the best. They couldn't keep hiding like this forever.

After that, Linda and Diane became best friends. For Linda, it was like having Jan back. The time she spent with Diane during the day was the only thing that got her through the nights with Donald. David had custody of the kids and Diane was living off base, alone in a house paid for by the support she received from David. Though watching her friend go through a divorce was hard, from the outside looking in, Diane's situation seemed perfect to Linda.

She was at the kitchen table folding clothes, daydreaming about life without Donald when he walked in, allowing the screen door to slam, which made her jump.

Donald said, "We need to talk."

Oh my God, what now? she thought. While she waited for Donald to speak, she lit a cigarette, wondering if maybe he was gonna ask her for a divorce.

"I'm listenin'," Linda said.

By the look on his face, apparently happy about it, Donald said, "I'm going back to Vietnam."

Confused, Linda asked, "Excuse me?"

Repeating himself, Donald said, "I am going back to Vietnam."

"I am confused. Why would they send you back to Vietnam?" Linda asked.

"They aren't sending me. I volunteered," Donald answered.

Linda listened as Donald explained how he felt it was his duty to serve his country. How it was his duty to protect the citizens of the United States of America from foreign threats.

"That's bullshit and you know it," Linda whispered as the veins on Donald's neck bulged and his face turned red. "I don't believe for a minute you're going back to Vietnam because you feel it's your duty to serve and protect."

"I'm going back to defend my country," Donald said adamantly.

"Really? I think there's another reason," Linda said.

"Like what?" Donald asked.

Answering his question, Linda said, "It's obvious you ain't been right since you got back. You've been like a carnival ride. One day you're up and the next you're down. And you're hiding from your family. I don't think you need to go back to Vietnam. I think you need help."

Donald's face got redder. "What're you saying?" he asked.

"I'm saying you need professional help, Donald." Reminding him of her past, she said, "You know, like the help you insisted I get."

"I don't need a sanitarium," Donald insisted.

"I didn't say you need a sanitarium. What I said was you need professional help. Donald, you need to talk to someone," Linda said.

"You're wrong. I am fine. I don't need to talk to anyone," Donald said.

"Then tell me the truth. Why are you goin' back to Vietnam?" Linda demanded.

Their arguing raged on and on until finally, Donald yelled, "OKAY, you want the truth? The truth is... I just can't." Stopping in mid-sentence.

Linda knew exactly what he was going to say, but she needed to hear him say it. "You can't what?" she asked.

Donald's posture changed. His eyes turned sad again and his shoulders slumped when he said, "I thought I could do this. I can't."

Again, knowing but needing to hear it, she asked, "You thought you could do what?"

"Okay, you want the truth. Here it is. I thought I could deal with the fact my wife had another man's baby. I can't. It was hard enough when David and Diane found out, and now my family just keeps calling. What am I supposed to say to them?" Donald asked.

The truth didn't surprise her. If Linda was in Donald's shoes, she wasn't sure what she'd do either. "When are you leavin'?" she asked.

"I leave in a month. I'm on leave now to settle my affairs," Donald said.

The time had come, and Linda knew it, so she said, "I think you should leave now. You've got no affairs to settle here."

"What do you mean, I should leave now?" Donald asked.

"It means just what I said. You should go now," Linda answered.

"And where should I go?" Donald asked.

"I don't care where you go, just go," Linda said.

"Honey," Donald said, "we need to talk about this."

"What is there to talk about? You've already made your decisions. You said you're leavin,' so GO!" she yelled, "GO NOW!"

Out of the corner of her eye, Linda saw Gina walk in the front door, cover her ears, and run to her bedroom.

"What will you do?" he asked.

"I've got no idea, but I'll figure somethin' out. And what the hell do you care, anyway? You up and volunteer to leave me and the girls and now you act like you're concerned for us? Don't worry, we'll be fine. Please just go," Linda said.

"Linda, please," Donald said, reaching out to grab her arm.

Pulling away, she said, "If it's true, you can't do this, then take your shit and go."

When Donald didn't move, Linda screamed, "GET OUT!"

The vibration from the bedroom door slamming shook the house. It scared Kiana, making her cry. Picking her up, Linda walked across the hall to check on Gina, who was hiding in her closet, crying.

Sounding very grown up, Gina asked, "Is daddy really leaving Momma?"

Linda said, "Yes, your daddy's goin' back to Vietnam."

Crying, Gina asked, "Why is he leaving? He just got home."

Linda said, "Gina Marie, you're gonna need to be a good girl now.

With your daddy leaving, I'm gonna need your help takin' care of your sister."

Gina asked again, "Why is my daddy leavin'?"

"If you wanna know why your daddy's leavin', ask him. All I know is, he's leavin', and I need to figure out what we're gonna do," Linda said.

"I heard you tell him to go. It's your fault he's leaving," Gina yelled.

"You're right. You heard me tell your daddy to leave, but you're five years old, young lady, and there are things you don't understand and right now I need you to be a good girl. Can you do that?" Linda asked.

"I'll be a good, just promise you won't leave me, too," Gina said.

Linda was about to console Gina when she heard the sound of breaking glass. Putting Kiana down on the floor, she said to Gina, "Your sister's diaper is wet. Please, change it."

Linda watched as Gina dried her eyes, took Kiana by the hand, and led her sister across the hall toward her bedroom.

Without A Goodbye

Within the hour, Donald walked out the door carrying his duffle bag, fishing rod, and a tackle box. Linda and Gina watched from the front window as Donald threw his stuff in the back seat of David's car. He turned briefly, looked at Gina waving at him with tears running down her face. Briefly looking at Linda, Donald turned and climbed into the front seat of the car.

Linda stared at the spot where moments before Donald stood, listening to the sound of David's car as it got further and further away until she could no longer hear it. It reminded her of the night in Hawaii when she'd watched him disappear into the night. Unlike then, now Linda wasn't worried if she'd ever see him again. This time, she bowed her head, praying she'd never see him again.

She knew Donald wasn't coming back, but just in case, Linda locked the door and drew the drapes, preferring the darkness.

After cleaning up the glass from the mirror Donald broke, she fed and bathed both girls, and tucked them into bed. Then, picking up pen and paper, Linda began writing. And what she wrote was a song, her song. A song she was certain one day would be a hit.

The following week, Linda's prayers were answered, and Donald shipped out.

Disgusted with Donald and all things military, Linda packed what she could in their car, withdrew what little money was in the bank, and moved in with Diane. With the cash, she paid Diane some rent and bought groceries. And with the car, she looked for work.

Now in her mid-twenties, with no diploma and no skills to speak of, once again Linda was alone. Except now she had two girls.

* * *

It was a full two weeks later when, frustrated, exhausted, and thirsty, Linda stepped into Wild Bill's Beer Bar. It was dark and damp and just the kind of place she needed to sit and feel sorry for herself.

She ordered a beer at the bar, letting her mind wander back to the day she'd walked into the Tiki Room for the first time and ordered beer. It seemed like such a long time ago. She took a cigarette out of her purse and was searching for a light when she heard a deep voice say, "Ma'am." She turned her head toward the sound of the voice and found a lit match held by a handsome cowboy.

"Thank you," Linda said, touching her cigarette to the flame of the match.

Blowing out the match, the cowboy whistled at the bartender, ordering two more beers saying, "Wild Bill, at your service."

"Hello, Mr. Wild Bill," Linda said, "and thank you again, but really, I only got time for one beer. I gotta go pick up my daughter from school," Linda said.

Laughing, Wild Bill said, "Oh, a housewife. Tell me what's brought you out of your husband's nest today and into mine?"

Linda grabbed her purse, intending to leave, but first she said, "And for your information Mr. Bill, I ain't gotta husband anymore. And I wasn't runnin' to your nest or anyone else's. I was out lookin' for a job so I can feed my two babies when I got thirsty, and so I stopped in for a beer."

The look on Bill's face told her he was genuinely sorry he'd offended her. "I beg your pardon, ma'am," he said, sliding the beer in her direction.

Before Linda knew it, she had consumed both beers and was late picking up Gina. Popping a mint in her mouth, she put on fresh lipstick and headed toward Gina's kindergarten classroom, determined not to feel too bad. After all, she'd gotten a job. Linda was now Wild Bill's newest cocktail waitress.

* * *

Seeing the frown on Gina's teacher's face, Linda made up a quick story explaining why she was late, then hustled Gina out the door.

In a hurry to tell Diane about her new job, Linda ran a red light and, the next thing she knew, there were flashing red lights in her rearview mirror. While she waited for the officer to approach, she looked at herself in the mirror, pressing her lips together to refresh her lipstick, glad she wore the blue floral dress she'd bought in Hawaii. The dress fit looser then, now it fit snuggly, in all the right places.

"Good afternoon, ma'am," the officer said as he approached the car.

Faking a slight blush, Linda said, "Hello, is everything okay?"

"I don't know, ma'am. I pulled you over because you ran a red light. Didn't you see the red light?" the officer asked.

"Yes sir," Linda answered. "I saw the light was red. I'm kinda in a hurry to get home, but I promise you I looked both ways before I went."

"So, you looked first, then ran the red light?" the officer asked.

"Yes, it's like I said. I'm in a bit of a hurry," Linda answered.

"I see. Have you been drinking today, ma'am?" the officer asked.

"What? No, of course not," Linda lied. "I just picked up my daughter from school and I was in a hurry to get home." Then she started crying and before she knew it, a story just rolled off her tongue.

"You see, officer, I got a call that my baby has a high fever and may need to go to the hospital."

"I'm terribly sorry, ma'am. Okay, I'm going to let you go with a warning today. No more running red lights. Deliberately or not," he said.

"Yes, sir," Linda said, drying her eyes. As she pulled away from the curb, her heart beat so fast she thought she was going to be sick.

"Momma, what's wrong with Kiana?" Gina asked with tears in her eyes.

Linda had completely forgotten Gina was in the car and knew she should be ashamed of herself for lying in front of her.

However, if I hadn't, she reasoned, *he might've given me a ticket, or worse,* she thought, *put me in jail. After all, I had just picked up Gina, I do need to get home, And I admitted to running the red light.* So, feeling completely justified, Linda turned to Gina and said, "Nothin' is wrong with Kiana."

"I heard you say your baby is sick, Momma," Gina insisted.

"Yes," Linda agreed, "you're right, I told the nice officer my baby was sick, but I need to get home because Diane is waiting for the car."

"Why didn't you tell him that, Momma?" Gina asked.

"Because I thought he was gonna put me in jail," Linda answered.

"Why would he do that?" Gina asked.

The ease with which she told two lies in two minutes concerned her, but having no excuse for herself, Linda said, "Oh, for goodness' sake, Gina Marie, you ask too many questions. I swear you wear me out."

Changing the subject, Gina asked, "Momma, do you want to know what we learned in kindergarten today?"

"You bet I do," Linda answered.

In the driveway, thankful Gina seemed to have forgotten about the officer and her lie, she saw Diane on the porch, pacing back and forth, crying.

As she got out of the car, Linda asked, "Diane, what's wrong?"

When Diane didn't answer, frantically Linda asked again. "Diane, what happened? Why are you crying?"

"Nothing happened," Diane answered hiccupping. "I was just worried about you. Where have you been?" she demanded. "I expected you home thirty minutes ago."

"Oh, dear God, Diane. I thought something was seriously wrong. I'm sorry I am late, but I got pulled over for running a red light and I had to lie my way out of a ticket," she explained. "Guess what, though? I got a job. I start tonight."

Working as a cocktail waitress wasn't the job she would've chosen. The pay was terrible, but the tips helped and for now it was all she had.

Had Linda been given a choice, she'd be singing on the stage at Wild Bill's as part of the band. She'd even learned every song in every set Wild Bill's band played by heart.

And although she didn't know how it was going to happen, Linda knew one day she was going to be singing up on the Wild Bill's stage. While she waited, she spent her nights happily singing and dancing from table to table, delivering drinks.

To entertain herself, Linda began doing what her daddy called spinning yarns. She likened the phrase spinning yarns to telling lies.

Like, when someone asked her where she was from, she told them she was from Nashville, where she'd sung back up for Loretta Lynn.

And when they asked her what brought her to their small town, Linda answered in her best southern drawl, "It's 'cause I fell in love with the most handsome cowboy I'd ever seen, of course."

"Ya see," she'd say, "he told me he worked a cattle ranch the size of a small town and begged me to come to California with him. I thought he wanted to marry me, so I followed him out here. Turns out I misunderstood, though. The truth was, he worked on a cattle ranch in a small town. And mostly, he just wanted someone to take care of him."

No matter what question they asked or what yarn she spun, she'd always ended by saying, "So here I am, BUT someday I'm gonna be back up singin' on the stage."

Billy was the only person who knew the truth, and the lies seemed so much more exciting to her than reality.

* * *

That Diane didn't love her working in a bar didn't bother Linda at all. And mostly, she ignored Diane's comments until the day she asked, "What would Donald say if he knew you were working in a bar?"

To which Linda answered, "Honestly, Diane, I don't give a rat's ass what Donald thinks about anything, and he doesn't need to know either 'cause it ain't none of his gosh dang business. He's the one who left. Trust me, I don't like it any more than you do, but right now I need this job. I've got kids to feed."

"You do know there's money in your bank account, right?" Diane asked.

No, she didn't know it and wondered how Diane did, but didn't ask.

"I'm sorry. I didn't mean to upset you. David and I are just concerned about you. We love you and the girls," Diane said.

"Listen Diane, I'm serious. I don't want you tellin' David or Donald anything about me or my girls," Linda said.

"In my defense, I didn't volunteer the information. David saw you at Wild Bill's and was worried about you. So, when he asked me about it, I told him he had no reason to worry and you were working at Wild Bill's until you found a better job," Diane explained. "That's when David told me Donald has been putting money in the bank for you every month. So, see, you don't need to work anymore," Diane said. "You can stay home and take care of your girls yourself."

Angry, Linda answered, "Listen, as far as I'm concerned, Diane, that's what I'm doin'. I'm takin' care of my girls myself. The money in the account is Donald's and I ain't gonna touch a dime of it," Linda said. "How about I tell you somethin' you can tell David. You tell him to tell Donald he can shove his money where the sun don't shine!"

"Someday you may need the money," Diane said. "Maybe you could think of it as a savings account. It's just sitting there growing each month and you won't touch it. Unless you need to," she added.

"Okay fine," Linda said, but I'm tellin' you I've got no intention of using a dime of his money. Not now. Not ever. Besides, I may be gettin' a new position at the bar."

Laughing, Diane asked, "Really? What position? There are only two positions there, yours and the bartender's, and we both know you can't work behind the bar. You're too short to see over the dang thing."

"Yes, really," Linda answered. "I can't say what it is yet, but I'll tell you this. It's more money and I won't be workin' as hard."

"And I'm sure your new friendship with Billy doesn't have a thing to do with you getting this new position either, does it?" Diane asked as she walked away.

Linda heard Diane's comment but ignored it. She knew she was just jealous because Linda had a job and a male friend and Diane had neither.

* * *

Two weeks later, Linda sat in the back of the bar in a dark corner listening intently as Trish, the lead singer of the Wild Bill's Band, auditioned singers for a recently vacated backup singer position.

As Linda listened to singer after singer audition, she was certain she had as good a chance as any of them. They were good, but she felt she was better.

Finally, her name was called. Standing up on trembling legs, she looked up at Billy sitting at the bar and smiled at him.

This was her shot, and she wasn't gonna miss it.

Linda walked up on the stage like she owned the thing.

Trish asked, "Are you ready Linda?"

"I'm ready, Trish. What shall I sing?"

"How about 'I Don't Wanna Play House?' by Tammy Wynette. Do you know it, or do you need the words?" Trish asked.

"Oh. I know it. Trust me, I know it by heart." Linda answered.

Linda took a deep breath, pulling the song deep into her heart.

Did she know it? Hell, she could've written it. She was certain, in fact, they'd written this song about her. About Linda's life, her little girl, and Donald. The words depicting Gina's sad observations, Linda's tears, and Donald's goodbyes.

"OK, then. When you're ready, just give a nod," Trish said.

Picking up the microphone, Linda nodded to the pianist, rocking back and forth with the beat. Closing her eyes, they filled with tears, as scenes from the last ten years passed before them.

She sang the song from the depths of her soul. Sad but certain her life could only get better, Linda sang the chorus, repeated the last verse, and ended on a perfect note.

Right there, at that very moment, Linda knew she was born to sing.

* * *

And even though Linda felt confident she'd get the backup singer position, when the call came, she was shocked.

The Final Betrayal

Four months later, Linda sat naked and happy in Billy's bed. She knew Wild Bill's was only a small stage in a small town in the middle of nowhere, still she was singing on a stage and to her, that was what mattered.

She and Billy had been seeing each other almost daily since the day of her audition. They were hot and heavy, and everyone knew about it because neither of them tried to hide it.

Linda didn't know how Billy felt about the fact she was married, but as far as Linda was concerned, she and Donald were as good as divorced. And she knew one day soon, she'd get around to getting the piece of paper to prove it.

In her opinion, Donald was the one who abandoned her. He'd tucked his tail between his legs and ran as fast and as far away as he could.

Unlike Donald, Billy was good to her. He bought her clothes and took her to nice places. He told her she was a star and even offered to finance her career if she moved to Nashville with him. And though the idea excited her, for now, Linda was happy right where she was.

At home, things hadn't gotten any better. Diane hadn't found a job and because Linda was on a six-month probation with the band, she continued to work as a cocktail waitress during the day and sang at night, which left Diane taking care of Gina and Kiana most of the time.

"Whatever happened to, 'I'll make more money and I won't be working as much?'" Diane asked.

Linda explained for the hundredth time why she needed to keep her cocktail waitress job. "You know, it's just until I am sure I'm in the band. What if it doesn't work out? I'll need my cocktail waitress job to go back to," Linda said.

"Oh, for God's sakes, you know Billy isn't going to fire you," Diane argued.

"He could," Linda said, "and then I wouldn't have a job. So, until then, I'm gonna keep workin'," Linda said. Then smiling sweetly, she added, "And you're better with my girls than I am. They love you."

"They love you, too. And they miss you when you're gone," Diane said.

"I doubt it. I see the look in Gina's eyes. She hates me now. She's outright mean and argues with me all the time. I know she blames me for Donald going away. It's him she misses, not me," Linda said.

"I don't think that's true. Gina adores you," Diane said.

"Well, true or not," Linda said, "I'm sorry it has to be this way, and I promise, as soon as my probation is up, I'll quit my day job."

And if Diane nagging her to quit her job and Gina arguing with her constantly wasn't enough, when Linda had a day off, Billy wanted her to spend it with him, even offering to spend the day with her and her girls.

Certain she wouldn't be happy seeing her momma with anyone other than her daddy, Linda hadn't told Gina about Billy, yet. Worrying she was going to lose Billy though, Linda finally invited him to dinner, then fretted for days over how to tell Gina about him and the dinner date.

Linda was in the bathroom, hurrying to put on her mascara because Billy would be there any minute. Out of time, she called Gina into the bathroom.

Sounding more like Diane than the five-year-old she was, Gina asked, "Where are you going now?"

Linda answered, "I'm ain't goin' anywhere. We're having company for dinner, though. So I need you to go put on your pretty pink dress."

Putting the toilet seat down and climbing up on it to watch Linda put on her makeup. Gina asked, "Who?"

"His name is Billy," Linda answered.

"Who is Billy?" Gina asked. "And why do I have to wear a dress?"

"Because I asked you to, Gina. Now please go put it on," Linda answered.

"Who else is coming?" Gina asked.

Frustrated with all of Gina's questions but knowing the last thing she needed was a fight with Gina just before Billy got there, she answered saying, "No one. Billy is my boss, and I've invited him over for dinner tonight, so I need you to put on your pink dress and be on your best behavior. Is that understood?"

"Okay, Gina answered, but after, can I play outside with Susan? We're trying to see who can catch the most lizards." Smiling, she added, "So far, I'm winning."

Then she watched as the smile on Gina's face faded and her eyes get sad, when Linda answered, "Yes. Later, right now, I need your help with Kiana." Linda knew better than anyone she asked a lot of her five-year-old daughter, but what other choice did she have?

Billy arrived right on time with flowers for her and a bag of licorice for Gina. Diane was out for the night with her kids, so they were alone. Gina was on her best behavior, as talkative as ever, and full of questions. She asked where Billy lived. If he had kids? Why did he own a bar? And asked if she could see it one day.

Laughing, Billy answered only Gina's last question, telling her yes, she could come and see his bar someday, which seemed to make her happy.

After dinner, Gina asked, "Momma, can I spend the night at Susan's?"

"Sure," Linda said. "Run and get some pajamas and I'll walk you over."

After taking Gina to Susan's, Linda put Kiana to bed. With Diane gone, Kiana asleep and Gina safely next door, she and Billy had the perfect opportunity to make up for some lost time. Desperate for each other, they made love on the living room couch, falling asleep in each other's arms.

A short time later, Linda woke up with Gina shaking her. Handing her a blanket, Gina said, "Momma, cover your breast."

Mortified, Linda did her best to cover herself with the tiny blanket while asking Gina why she wasn't at Susan's house.

"I woke up scared, so I walked home," Gina said.

Billy woke up and tried to sit up. Linda pushed him back down. Turning back to Gina, she said, "Okay, go climb into my bed and I'll be there in a minute."

"Okay Momma." Then turning, she smiled and said, "Goodbye, Billy."

* * *

Linda had been singing backup with Wild Bill's Band for six months when her big break finally came. Trisha came down sick with laryngitis, and frantic to find another lead singer, Billy called, asking if she could sing lead until Trish got better.

"Are you serious? YES! YES, I would love to!" Linda screamed. Then, hanging up the phone, she ran to tell Diane her good news. Diane wasn't as happy about Linda's news as Linda was, and they got into another fight.

"I think this Billy guy is just using you," Diane stated flatly.

"Really, and just what is he usin' me for?" Linda asked.

"What *isn't* he using you for? If he needs someone to wait on tables, he calls you. And now he needs someone to sing, so he calls you. Oh, and when he needs a piece of ass, you know, he calls you," Diana answered.

"Hey, you wait a gosh darn minute. What the hell makes you think you can talk to me like that?" Linda yelled.

Diane yelled back, "I think I can talk to you like that because I'm the one here cleaning the house, doing laundry, shopping, cooking and raising your kids."

Laughing, Linda said, "Jesus, Diane, you sound like a jealous lover."

"You laugh," Diane said, "but let me ask you something. When was the last time you picked Gina up from school or changed Kiana's diaper?"

Linda couldn't deny it. Diane was right, so she didn't answer.

"You're never here anymore. And when do you plan to talk to Gina about what she saw on the couch the other night?" Diane asked.

Again, Diane was right and Linda was ashamed of herself. Not knowing what to say to Gina, she'd ignored it entirely.

"Diane, I'm sorry you feel like your raisin' my kids and I know I need to talk to Gina about what she saw, and I will," Linda promised. "And since I'm off probation, I plan on quitting my cocktail waitressing job, like I promised. So, I'll be around the house more to help with the kids. Hey, I heard there's a new Disney movie coming out soon. How about we take the kids to see it?" Linda suggested.

"How about we go out alone?" Diane suggested.

Seeing the pleading look in Diane's eyes, Linda asked, "You wanna go to a Disney movie alone?" Linda asked.

"Not really, but if it is the best you have to offer, I'll take it," Diane answered.

"Good," Linda said. "Now, I need to get to the bar and rehearse with the band. I ain't never sung lead before and I'm so nervous," Linda said. "We'll go out next week, just the two of us, I promise."

Driving to the bar, Linda thought about her conversation with Diane. She knew better than anyone Diane deserved a night out without the girls. So, when she got to the bar, she walked straight to the phone and called home, inviting Diane to come see her sing one night soon. Promising she'd even find the babysitter.

As Linda hung up, Billy walked in carrying a clothes bag. Kissing her, he said, "I've got a present for you, if you're interested?"

Linda's eyes twinkled with excitement as she opened the clothes bag to find the prettiest dress she'd ever seen. It was black, short, silky, low cut and covered in sequins. Linda was thrilled.

"Billy, it's the most beautiful thing I've ever seen and I wanna try it on in the worst way, but I need to practice with the band right now." Looking around, she asked, "Are they here yet?"

"No, I asked them to give you a couple of hours to pull yourself together. They'll be here at five."

Linda panicked. Laughing, Billy insisted she'd have plenty of time to rehearse. Pressing her body up against his, Linda purred, asking, "What am I gonna do in the meantime?" she asked.

Handing her the clothing bag, Billy said, "I got a few ideas. For starters, how about you go try this dress on?"

An hour later, Linda, smiling from ear to ear and wrapped in a white cotton sheet, naked and happy, she stared at the black dress hanging at the other end of the room. The dress fit like a glove and she couldn't wait to stand center stage wearing the sexiest dress she'd ever seen and sing her heart out.

Her first night singing lead was an experience she knew she'd never forget. And every night since had been even better than the one before and Linda knew deep down in her heart she could never give up center stage.

With Trisha due back at the end of the week, Linda was desperate. And although she knew the opportunity didn't really exist, she asked, "Billy, what would you say if I told you I was gonna try out to sing lead with another band when Trisha gets back?"

Rolling over and turning out the light, Billy answered, "I'd say no."

Turning the light back on, Linda said, "Wait a minute, I wanna talk to you."

He turned the light back off, saying, "There's nothing to talk about. You work here. For me."

Linda got up, put on her robe, and lit a cigarette. The dark helped, and Linda felt courageous saying, "Billy, you know I don't wanna work for anyone else either, but I can't give up the lead. It's always been my dream to sing on a stage. There's got to be a way," she pleaded.

Turning the light on again, Billy said, "Okay, if you're serious, there may be a way."

"I'm dead serious. Please tell me how," Linda asked.

"I've arranged for a talent scout to hear the band play, and if he likes what he hears, he may offer us an opportunity in Nashville. It's not a given, of course, but this band is good. The best one I've ever had," Billy said. "And now with you in it, it's great."

Pouting a bit, Linda asked, "With Trisha as lead?"

"Yes," Billy answered. "Trisha will sing lead, but if it works out, once we are in Nashville, we'll have a clear avenue to explore a solo career for you. Linda, you know I believe in you. Now come back to bed."

Her mind raced a mile a minute. There had to be another way and Linda was determined to find it, but for now, she felt it was better to play along. Crawling back into bed, she cuddled up next to Billy, kissed his neck sweetly, and said goodnight.

The following morning, Linda got up, dressed, and left before Billy woke up. When she got home, Diane was up, too, sitting at the kitchen table. "I didn't expect to see you so early today," Diane said sarcastically.

"I wanted to see Gina before she went to school," Linda lied. She hadn't slept a wink the night before and a plan was forming, but Linda needed time away from Billy and the bar to think it through. She might've convinced Billy she would give up the lead, however, knowing a talent scout was coming to town, there was no way in hell Linda was going to give up this chance. She just needed to figure out how to convince Billy to let her sing for the scout.

She was lying awake in her bed with Kiana cuddled up next to her, sleeping, when the answer came to her. Maybe, just maybe, she could convince Billy to let her sing a solo for the scout. She could sing her song. The one she'd written the night Donald left. Linda knew it was a long shot, but she had to try.

And to her amazement, Billy agreed without needing much convincing.

* * *

The weeks flew by and the band worked hard, rehearsing daily. Linda introduced the band to her original song and with a just a few tweaks, the band worked together to write the music. The outcome was a masterpiece and Linda knew it would catapult her to exactly where she was meant to be. And she wouldn't be standing to the left or to the right of Trish singing harmony anymore. She'd be standing center staged, singing her heart out just like she'd imagined all those years ago. *Finally, my dreams of singing on the big stage are comin' true,* Linda thought.

When the big night came, Billy gave permission for Diane to bring Gina to the bar to watch her perform.

Dressed in her black sequined dress and black silk stockings, Linda was pacing the floor barefoot nervously when Billy walked in.

"Dear God in heaven, Billy," Linda said. "I don't think I've ever been this nervous."

"You better swallow those nerves, little lady, cause this is it. You ready?" Billy asked.

Slipping into her shoes, she answered, "As ready as I'm ever gonna be."

The bright lights were her salvation. Center stage, unable to see a thing in front of her, with only her emotion to rely on, Linda sang her heart out. And when she finished, there wasn't a dry eye in the place and Linda's heart soared hearing Gina's voice in the audience screaming at the top of her lungs, "That's my momma. That's my momma."

* * *

The Wild Bill's Band was offered a gig at an up-and-coming Nashville nightclub for the summer, and if all went well, the promise of a recording contract.

After weeks of heated arguments about why Linda couldn't leave her girls behind to go to Nashville and Billy arguing about why she couldn't take them with her, the band left without her. Billy offered her old job back but distraught, Linda declined his offer and quit.

* * *

Resuming her position as a single and now an unemployed mother, Linda had just picked Gina up from school when she asked, "Momma, can I listen to the radio?"

"I suppose so," Linda answered, staring out at the road in front of her, thinking about Billy. He'd been gone months now and, so far, she hadn't heard from him, and she figured she probably wasn't going to either.

"Momma, listen!" Gina screamed. "It's your song."

Linda pulled over to a curb and turned up the volume. She listened in disbelief as Trisha belted out the words to her song. They'd changed the lyrics slightly. The melody was exactly the same.

Sitting on the side of the road, it only taken a split second for Linda to decide she was going to Nashville. Billy and the band had stolen her song, and she would not let it happen without a fight.

As the plan formed in her head, Linda said, "Gina, when school's out, how'd you like it if you and your sister went to stay with Grandma Irma for a while?"

"Why? Who's Grandma Irma and where are you going?" Gina asked.

"I'm goin' to New Orleans to the Mardi Gras," Linda lied.

*　*　*

Two weeks later, Linda withdrew every dime out of Donald's bank account. Then she loaded her car with as much of their belongings as she could. With Diane sitting in the passenger seat, Gina, and Kiana asleep in the back seat, Linda left Barstow and everything she owned behind.

Epilogue

The look on Gina's face the day she left was etched permanently in Linda's mind and no matter how much she drank, she couldn't forget it. The scene played out over and over in her head.

Her saying, "Gina, I'm gonna need you to be a good girl now. You need to help your grandma with your sister. I'll be back in two weeks."

And Gina's defiant face looking her right in the eye, saying, "No, you aren't. You aren't ever coming back, Momma."

She'd argued with Gina, insisting she was coming back, and Gina argued back, certain she wasn't.

And Gina was wrong. Linda came back. She came back three months later. Only to face the fact she'd truly lost everything.

* * *

In Nashville, Linda failed to get rights to her song because she could not prove she'd written it. Then, when she returned to California, she found her momma's house empty with the windows boarded up and her children nowhere to be found. Not knowing where else to go, Linda went to Mabel's house, hoping Gina and Kiana were there.

There, Linda was told that on the day her daddy served her momma divorce papers, her momma tried to commit suicide, almost killing herself and both girls. Not knowing what else to do, Mabel had called the Red Cross, who contacted Donald in Vietnam, informing him his wife had abandoned his children and they needed him at home.

"Where are Donald and the girls now?" Linda asked.

She could tell by the look on her sister's face what she was about to say would not be something she wanted to hear.

"Well, Mabel answered, "Donald is back in Vietnam."

"And the girls?" Linda asked.

When Mabel didn't answer, with tears forming in her eyes, Linda asked again, "Mabel, where are my girls?"

"Donald gave them to Lewis and Kaitlyn," Now crying herself, Mabel said, "Linda, I am so sorry. If I had thought for one minute Donald would have done something like that, I would never have called him."

* * *

The following day, Linda took the few dollars she'd borrowed from her sister and bought a one-way bus ticket to New Orleans, this time for real.

About the Author

Tina Katamay, grew up loving to read. As a teenager, she read books about love and heroism. Though they were fun books to read and fantasize about, there was never a divorce, there was plenty of money, and they always had a happy ending.

In Tina's case, this was not true. Her story is comprised of mental illnesses, abandonment, substance abuse, and even court custody battles. Yet, it is a beautiful story of *real life* without happy endings.

My Real Mother begins the story.

Tina is currently writing the sequels to *My Real Mother*. In *My Other Mother*, Tina focuses on love and loyalty *(expected release Spring 2025)*. In the third volume, *The Good Girl*, Tina contemplates forgiveness *(expected release Fall, 2025)*.

Tina is a wife, mother, and grandmother. She lives in Paso Robles, California, with her husband Roman, her daughter Amber, and her kitty, Pumpkin. In her spare time, Tina dabbles in interior and exterior design, travels whenever she can, and loves to cook and entertain.

Visit Tina's website at **www.tinankatamay.com**